THE
RECIPE
FOR BUSINESS SUCCESS

Curtis R. Nelson

ISBN 978-1-61623-035-7

Library of Congress catalog number is available upon request.

Although the author and publisher have made every effort to ensure the accuracy and completeness of information contained in this book, we assume no responsibility for errors, inaccuracies, omissions, or any inconsistency herein. The stories are presented for educational purposes and are not meant as historical accounts. Any slight of people, places, or organizations are unintentional.

First Printing 2009

Editor: Kristy Raine; Reference Librarian and Archivist, Mount Mercy College
Cover design and layout: Susan Larson; Art Director, Metro Studios

Attention Corporations, Organizations, Schools, and Universities:
Quantity discounts are available for bulk purchases for educational and gift purposes. Special books or book excerpts can also be created to fit special needs.

For information, please contact: CRN LLC, 3607 Timberline Drive NE, Cedar Rapids, Iowa, 52402 Ph: 319-329-7364 E-mail: curt@recipeforbusinesssuccess.com

*To my parents, Robert and Arline, for providing
the foundation and encouragement needed
to succeed in my early business years;*

*To my wife Lori and children Blake and Krista Shea,
for providing the love and support required
to realize ongoing success;*

*To the incredible teams of people with whom
it has been my great pleasure to jointly create
the many business successes of my life.*

PREFACE

This book is for all businesses. Participants, and readers, who are leading established companies, some as old as eighty years, tend to believe that "The Recipe for Business Success" discussed here must be targeted for start-ups or early-stage businesses. Surely the "Recipe" for an existing, established business must be far less extensive; in fact the "Recipe" for driving an existing, even very well established, business is exactly the same.

Changes in the market, from competition, to consumer trends, to the overall global environment, will continually challenge the status quo of even the most established business. Those that believe otherwise will simply fail to take advantage of opportunities and, more importantly, leave themselves open for "unexpected" impacts.

Business fundamentals are as necessary for the experienced player as they are for the novice. In an NFL training camp, all members of the team work on fundamentals each season. Tiger Woods still hits 1,000 golf balls every day, working on basics. Reviewing the fundamentals enables one to excel; the same is true in the business world.

There are many books dedicated to one specific business ingredient or an execution component. This text, however, is designed to help any business review its complete business "Recipe." It is organized to identify gaps, and, in an educated manner, help you gather and employ the ingredients and execution capabilities needed to improve.

It is my sincere hope that you take the time to use this

book as a guide to significantly improve your business success. I hope you dedicate this time to work "on" your business rather than "in" it and to honestly identify multiple opportunities for improvement.

Enjoy!

TABLE OF CONTENTS

INTRODUCTION

Since graduating with a marketing degree (BBA University of Iowa, 1974), I have enjoyed the challenges and excitement associated with creating and accelerating over forty five different global businesses in industries such as: communication, transportation, information technology, medicine, health and fitness, and lawn and garden. While building and leading teams since my early twenties, I have done many things right, and learned many lessons the hard way. In all that time, I have had the passion and drive to make things happen. Every career change has been challenging and exciting; I have learned from them all, good and bad.

Even in situations you do not like, where your business, or one in which you are working, is "doing it wrong" and getting away with it, you can still learn. In most cases, when someone wants to pay you to learn, you should take advantage of the opportunity. While sitting in a Wendy's® Restaurant in 1985, I sought counsel from a trusted advisor. An information communications business, a company I grew and in which I worked, had been sold to a competitor. The new owner needed the market footprint and brand recognition our business had achieved to expand its product depth and diversity. However, the competitor was a very old business with a science-based, very autocratic process and systems-driven culture. This dynamic was the antithesis of the entrepreneurial, market-driven personality that had made our business successful.

Sold with the deal, I was now challenged with the integration of both business teams, and the culture clash was explosive. I was lamenting about the situation to my advisor when he looked at me, over his habitual small bowl of Wendy's Chili, and said, "Are you learning anything?" That stopped my whining. Of course, I was learning all kinds of new things, many by experiencing how *not* to do them. I finished integrating those businesses as best I could and moved on to a new venture in the physical therapy industry, learning along the way.

It was later in my career, during a true "how not to do things" experience, that I started to document the real "Recipe" for a successful business. My responsibility was to drive market introduction and revenue growth for a new, long-haul trucking, wireless communications business inside a Fortune 500 technology contractor. Not only did we need to compete with a major competitor that had a multi-year jump on the market, but it was also necessary to help our business unit understand a commercial execution model with which it had little experience. To aid in that process, I found myself creating a written recipe that illustrated how a successful commercial enterprise looked and performed.

I chose the word "recipe" because all ingredients and execution requirements must be implemented in balance, and in order, to realize the desired outcome. While a business may be very strong in some areas, if it cannot execute a complete "Recipe," it will fall short of its potential or fail altogether. By this time in my career, I had significant experience in businesses having some strong components, but none that had really executed a balanced and complete "Recipe."

While documenting the elements, I was also helping a previous co-worker create a new business in the computer telephony (computer / telecommunications) industry. When it became clear that my Fortune 500 employer was not going to adopt the needed approach, and when it also became clear that the new computer company was perched at the beginning of a major change in the telecommunications industry, I resigned and embraced the new venture.

As a footnote, my Fortune 500 employer failed to achieve its goals with the trucking communications division, and within two years it was sold. You will read different stories in this book that demonstrate the reasons for such failure, and you will come to know that big or small, businesses can just as easily make serious "Recipe" mistakes and suffer accordingly.

Jumping from previous positions where my teams had numbered in the hundreds, to an early-stage technology company with fewer than twenty employees seemed risky. I remember my wife saying to me, "You are leaving your current position for a little computer company?" During my first couple of weeks, I sat on the floor in my office until I procured furniture. With this opportunity, I was excited to use the "Recipe" I had been learning and documenting to make this company a real success. From the consulting work I had performed during the start-up phase, I knew they had the first ingredient, a solid initial position in a fast-growing market.

The founder, who had been the chief engineer at one of my previous employers, said to me, "Well, you always said you knew how to grow a business if you could do it your way. I guess we are about to find out." He was a quality electrical engineer that had designed many successful products in his career, and he had taken the needed risk to start this business.

However, unlike many early-stage entrepreneurs, he was wise enough to know where he excelled and where he did not, and he allowed me to engage accordingly. I owe him a debt of gratitude for taking that risk and for providing me the opportunity to help create a company that was on Inc. Magazine's 500 Fastest Growing Private Companies® list three years in row (1997-1999). Unlike many who graced that list in the 1990s, we generated profits of 16% or more every one of those years.[1,2,3]

As a major provider of OEM (Original Equipment Manufacturer) and branded server communication products to the communications industry, we built a very successful manufacturing company. We created a strong global brand, and we funded our growth with company earnings, not venture capital. For these significant accomplishments, I credit an excellent team of people, another critical "Recipe" component that will be discussed.

Recipe for Business Success
When asked by a reporter in 1999 how our business had been successful enough to earn a spot on Inc. Magazine's list for three consecutive years, I provided the following analogy:

"It's like baking a cake. If you get the ingredients and execution right, success is easier to attain and sustain. We have been continually successful because we have combined great ingredients with great execution, and it has been no harder or easier than that."

This is not to say that a lot of very hard work did not go into that level of success, but no matter how hard we worked, if the ingredients and execution capabilities had not been what they were, the outcome would have been very different.

In 2001 the communications industry collapsed, significantly impacting revenue and operations, but due to the team in place, we turned in a positive year. That feat is one of which I am the most proud; others in that industry did not fare as well. Our accomplishments during a significant downturn were again directly the result of having the right "Recipe" at the right time.

Recipes Require Balance

In the culinary world, great results come from a quality recipe that includes the right balance of ingredients (quality and amount) and execution (guidance, talent and resources). Poor results come from inadequacies or lack of balance in any of these areas. The further "off recipe" you get, the worse the results - sometimes even inedible. The same is true in business; a successful "Recipe" balances quality ingredients with excellent execution.

Quality Ingredients for Quality Results

There are two key ingredients required for business success:
- A viable and defendable reason to be in business.
- A business plan that provides the architecture for success.

Just *wanting* to have a successful business is not sufficient. Just because you have been operating for many years and people have always purchased what you offer, does not mean the venture will continue. You must continually provide a product or service that solves a problem or satisfies a need so that people or businesses will exchange money for it. You must make money; if the same product or service is available from other sources, you must continually answer one question – why will they keep buying yours?

You must also be able to specifically identify a target market that is large enough and reachable enough to provide acceptable revenue. In other words, you need to have a defined

THE RECIPE FOR BUSINESS SUCCESS

"Fit" in the marketplace, whether you are just getting started or have been in business for decades. My experience as a consultant and executive coach with hundreds of early-stage and established businesses has taught me that this ingredient is the most overlooked. Entrepreneurs start businesses because they can, not always because they should. Established businesses continue for the same reason, and thus, many have offerings that do not line up with market demand, even if such needs had been there in the past. These companies become a business in search of a market, instead of the other way around.

Presuming you can identify a defendable and viable reason to be in business (Strategic Fit), you need to create a quality plan to capitalize on that market "Fit."

- What is your long-term mission?
  - How will you know if you are achieving it?
- What kind of culture will you need?
  - How will you create and maintain it?
- What assumptions must you make?
  - How will you react if they are not correct?
- What are your goals?
  - Are they measurable and achievable?
- What are your strengths and weaknesses?
  - Have you been honest? Can you capitalize on them?
- What is your marketing plan?
  - Is it based upon a strong foundation?
- What are your operational plans?
  - Will they provide value to your customers and your business?
- What resources are necessary?
  - How will you get them?

- When will you take action?
  - Who will be held responsible?
- How will you monitor your success and your industry's evolution?
  - Will you take the needed time to work "on" your business regularly?

A good business plan is the foundation of your success; proceeding without one is a big mistake!

Execution - Making it Happen

A great "Fit" and plan are of little value if a business cannot execute effectively. Viable businesses fail on a regular basis simply from lack of, or poor, execution. Quality execution is a combination of three things:

- Talent
- Leadership
- Resources

The right business talent means assembling people with applicable experience and needed capabilities in all major disciplines – marketing, development, sales, operations, information technology (IT) and finance. It also means finding talent that has common goals, aspirations, and working styles so they can execute and win as a team. Far too many businesses have had a great product and failed because personnel were poorly matched and balanced, or because they could never work as a team. In today's competitive environment, it takes significantly more than a great product offering to succeed.

Proper guidance comes from quality leadership. It takes a great leader to assemble the right ingredients, to gather the best talent and resources, to provide a clear roadmap, and to create the culture necessary for success. Nearly everyone can recount the effects of a poor leader on a business and on the company's ability to be successful.

Ultimately, to have a successful business you need the proper resources. These essentials include adequate funding, tools, information, personnel and working environment ideally all matched appropriately to your plan. Having more or less of any resource than needed will impact your ability to succeed. Not enough capital? Wrong location? Bad data? Shortage of qualified personnel? All lead to poor execution.

No Mystery to Success
There is no mystery to business success. There are no magic pills or trendy philosophies that make one company better than another. In the business world, quality results come from quality execution with the right ingredients. It has never been any easier, or any harder, than that. Businesses that are out of balance can operate without ever understanding or identifying the related opportunities to improve. Many attain less than half of their potential while considering themselves a success. Some struggle for years.

Other businesses succeed in spite of themselves simply because of unique and supporting market dynamics. If you have the only restaurant and source of food on a well inhabited island, you can serve poor food, abuse your customer base, and still come to believe that you are a great business person because people keep coming back. A real business person will identify the strategic opportunity to provide better food and service and put your poor efforts out of business. In all likelihood, you will blame your subsequent failure on the competition, instead of your "Recipe."

INTRODUCTION

Many, if not most, businesses that have failed did not understand that not recognizing or addressing serious gaps in their own ingredients and execution caused their failure. These companies adopted the "it's not my fault – it's the market's fault" mentality, rather than truly understanding or recognizing the gaps in their "Recipe."

This book explains the key ingredients and execution requirements necessary to create and to maintain a successful business. The book provides a "Report Card" that allows you to score your business against the material presented. In the process, you will likely learn that you are missing required ingredient and execution components, and you may realize that you are "out-of-balance." I sincerely hope you will see the gaps identified as opportunities to improve both your business and your professional performance.

Getting the most out of The Recipe for Business Success
In this book you will find detailed information to help you:
- Define a viable and defendable "Fit" in the market place.
- Write a business plan that will drive success.
- Build a team with the right talent in the right places.
- Improve your business' leadership.
- Secure and balance the resources needed to win.

With the provided content and supporting resources, you will be able to use this book as a daily guide to improved performance. The supporting resources have been used successfully, many for decades, and they are available on our website at http://www.recipeforbusinesssuccess.com.

If you use this book to build the "Recipe" for your business success, it will not be long before you realize that running a successful business really can be as easy as "baking a cake."

THE RIGHT INGREDIENTS

STRATEGIC FIT
A Viable Reason to be in Business

"Strategic Fit" defines the viable reason(s) why your business can be successful, and denotes the foundational component of your business planning process.

The wrong reasons to start a business are because you want to do so, or it sounds fun, that you cannot work for anyone else, or that you invented something your friends think is "cool." These might be good reasons to start assessing the potential for a business, but they are not adequate to begin execution. If you already operate a business, it is wrong to always assume the same focus because of past success, which is not a guarantee of future prosperity. Ongoing gains are only partially impacted by your history. Previously strong businesses fail on a regular basis because they lost track of, or never really understood, why they were successful in the first place.

The right reason to be in business is because an opportunity exists to provide a product or a service for a definable set of customers, who will consistently buy from you, in adequate volumes, at profitable margins. There is not always room for additional competition, but there is always room for a business that solves a real need or a problem for which buyers are willing to pay. Such a business has a "Strategic Fit."

Do the Hard Work
To aim your business in the right direction, you must deter-

mine if there is truly an ongoing viable need for **_your_** offering in the marketplace. You will need to conduct an in-depth "Fit" analysis. Many textbooks and plan outlines commonly call this a "situation analysis." It is critical to understand the market and industry situation, and to also have a clear understanding of how you can, and will, address these dynamics before moving forward, hence a "Strategic Fit" analysis.

By understanding the entire landscape in which you will be, or are conducting business, as well as your ability to provide a viable product that will generate profit, you will understand why, where and how your business can be successful. Skipping this essential step, or making false assumptions to avoid the work, is like leaving out a baking ingredient because you had none and did not want to go to the store. This step is hard work when done correctly; if it is omitted, success is left to chance.

New businesses that skip this crucial step have very high failure rates because many of them simply had no viable reason to start operating. Similarly, once successful businesses are frequently guilty of failing to keep their "Strategic Fit" analysis up to date and fail to evolve effectively. From my experience, skipping this step is why the failure rate for new businesses is greater than fifty percent. It is also the reason why once successful businesses fail to effectively evolve or simply fail altogether. Had they done their research, owners could have saved their investments and friendships, could have effectively evolved and created new jobs, and could have avoided the heartache of failure.

To determine if there is a "Fit" for your business, at a minimum, you should be able to answer these questions:
- Is there a real need for what my business offers?

- Can the need be independently validated?
- Is there a viable opportunity for the offering?
  - Who are the target buyers and what are they like?
  - Where are they and can you reach them?
  - Are there enough of them?
  - Who is the competition?
  - Can you defend your position?
- Can you produce the right product for the opportunity?
  - Can you meet the defined need?
- Can you price the product to sell and still make a profit?
  - Will your price also create differentiation?
- Can you produce and deliver the product as needed and promised?
  - Will you manufacture internally or outsource production?
- Will the overall market environment support or hinder your success?
  - How will you monitor these dynamics?

Does Anyone Want What You Provide?

Foundationally, you must first determine if there is a viable need for what you provide in the market. Do you solve a problem that customers are willing to pay to have solved? This may sound obvious, but there are thousands of products developed annually that 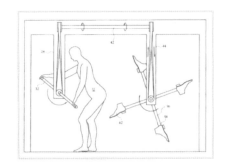 only solve problems in the inventor's mind.

Take for example US Patent # 6,293,874.[4] The inventor designed a device that allows the user to kick his own buttocks. I am sure that at some point the creator imagined there was a need for such a product (due to the trouble and expense of obtaining a patent) but you are probably smiling, wondering who might actually pay for such a device – especially at the price it would likely take to be profitable.

Defining a viable need has everything to do with the problem your product solves or the need it fulfills. The more intense the need, the easier and faster a prospective buyer will part with money to purchase a solution. The larger the cost of the problem, the more money a customer will pay. Commonly called a "Need Analysis," this study is a critical first step in validating a successful business.

The following, simple chart allows a better understanding of the concept. As the intensity of need increases, the amount of sales and marketing effort required to cause a customer to buy is reduced.

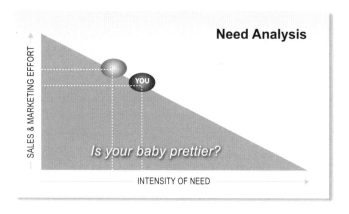

An example: If you developed a pill that was found to cure any form of cancer, the intensity of need would be at the maximum because the drug would save lives and there would be no known competition. The sales and marketing investment necessary to create demand would be near zero. A single press release would generate all the demand your business could endure. If, on the other hand, you have just created a new #2 lead pencil, the intensity of need would clearly be much lower, and the competition much higher. Consequently, the investment needed to generate adequate revenue would be significantly greater.

Taking the time to accurately position a product on this chart will help you understand its viability as well as the amount of resources needed to invest in the sale. The lower the need, or the perceived need for the product, the more difficult success becomes. In many cases, businesses that may have been successful fail simply because they did not invest the capital necessary to generate demand.

Don't guess. Conduct your own secondary or primary research, or buy the research you need from qualified vendors, and then make fact-based decisions. If you are, right now, mentally or physically marking yourself on the chart, ask yourself what factual evidence you have to support that position. If you cannot validate the reasoning independently, you could be very mistaken and therefore, be making poor decisions.

If there is a definable need for the product, a need that has been validated by current competitors, you must understand why there is a need for _your_ product. Is there a problem that the competitors do not solve? Is there a price or benefit position currently not being served? Is there a location or market segment that is not being served?

If you are operating a business and there is additional competition entering your market, do they know things you do not? Should you be making proactive decisions to stay ahead? If your business has stopped growing or is declining, do you know why? Should you be finding new customers? Providing new products? Dropping old products? Should you be moving in new or different directions?

There is *not* always room for competition. You cannot always enter a market just because of personal interest. When a few friends think you have a novel idea, their opinions alone do not mean a product will sell.

Keep in mind the following analogy as you ask personal acquaintances about your ideas or current business. *When you have your first child and you show his/her picture to your friends and co-workers and say, "Isn't he / she cute," what do you think they are going to say? When you ask these same people about your company or business ideas, you will get similar responses, most being nice, not honest.*

If you are starting a new business, getting the analysis right is critical to your success. If you are in an active business which needs to perform better, the analysis may cause you to rethink and redirect your offerings.

If you can't define a viable market need for your product – stop and re-think your business. Do not create products in search of a market, and do not stay in business just because you have always been there.

RECIPE CHECK: STRATEGIC FIT

To validate the need for your business, at a minimum, you should be able to answer the following questions:

- Does your product solve a definable problem or fill a definable need?
  - If so, what is it?

- Can you define the cost (or pain) to your customer for the problem you are solving or the need you are filling?
- Are similar products already available and being purchased?
  - If so, how does yours differ?
  - Can you validate the need for the difference?

Who Wants What You Provide?

Once you have determined that a viable need exists, the next question to answer is whether the need is large enough to create, sustain, and / or grow a viable business. Just because a focus group's members said they would purchase the item, or because you have clients currently purchasing, does not mean there are enough customers to build or sustain the business you desire. Understanding who your target prospect is, the actual size of the market opportunity, and realistically estimating the amount of that market which you can capture or maintain with your product is the next step in your "Fit" analysis.

Many businesses start or persist with the attitude that since others are selling the same product and they provide a "better" option, there must be room for them as well – i.e., always room for competition. In situations where the business is a new category entrant (first to market) and no like offerings have ever been sold, many forge ahead with the belief that if a few buy the product now, many will buy it in the future. In all such cases, these assumptions are made without quality data, which means that businesses are simply guessing. That is not to say that one cannot guess correctly; many businesses have been created that way, using a good guess with good timing. However the odds are against it.

THE RECIPE FOR BUSINESS SUCCESS

Your odds of success will be significantly improved by:

- Knowing that you have an offering that will be adopted or will continue to be purchased over a predictable time period.
- Understanding specifically who your target customers are so that you can identify effective ways to reach them.
- Identifying that there is a large enough market for you to service.

If you continue to do this well over time, you will create a market leading, highly sustainable business that will long outlast your competition.

Who are your target prospects? Can you describe them demographically?

- For an individual buyer:
  - Gender
  - Age
  - Race
  - Income
  - Education
  - Employment status
- For a business:
  - Type
  - Size
  - Vitality

Can you describe your prospects psychographically?

- For an individual:
  - Personality
  - Values
  - Attitudes

- Interests
- Lifestyles
- For a business:
  - Culture
  - Values
  - Ethics

Can you describe your prospects geographically - where are they located?
- What city?
- What region?
- What country?

Can you describe the prospects' behaviors?
- Are they risk takers? Will they adopt new ideas readily?
- Are they conservative purchasers? Will they wait for others to adopt your product first?
- Will they use your product heavily or lightly?
- Are they price or value purchasers?
- Will they be high maintenance or low maintenance users?
- Will they change vendors easily or are they very loyal?

Far too many businesses make broad assumptions that overestimate or incorrectly identify an actual target buyer. This error causes poor projections, wasted or ineffective marketing and sales efforts, incorrectly designed offerings, limited growth, or even failure.

For an animal repellant business I started in the lawn and garden industry (RepelIT LLC – http://www.deerfortress.com), a test marketing program, secondary market research, and contracted primary market research were employed and revealed the following details. My target buyer was a female gardener, over fifty years of age, with an annual household income of $50,000 or more living in the United States. She had a college or advanced education degree. She was retired and spends, on average, $3,500 per year on plants and gardening supplies. There were 35 million such buyers available.

Knowing that information, I was able to more easily project the number of potential buyers and associated revenue, as well as to identify specific marketing and sales strategies to effectively reach these buyers. The ability to more easily design product offerings that continually matched up with buyer needs was improved. And yet, I would wager that many, if not most providers of gardening supplies, are far less accurate in their target identification, and as a result, their success suffers, whether they know it or not.

Describing your target buyer with such specifics still misses critical psychological and behavioral impacts that affect buying decisions. Buyer lifestyles, values, opinions, interests, behaviors, hobbies, status and other like impacts can and will change the actual identification and size of your available market. These factors will also significantly impact how and what you must communicate to effectively reach and maintain them. Typical questions you should be able to answer are:

- Do the actions of other people or businesses impact their buying decision?
- Do the target market members buy as a class or genre?
- Is function, style or brand more significant?
- What type of risk must a buyer take to purchase your offering? How does that effect their decisions?

Adoption Cycle
A classic marketing tool, the Adoption Cycle[5] helps you bet-

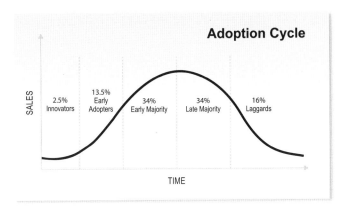

ter understand your target prospect's buying behavior. All buyers, whether they are buying for themselves, their families, or their businesses, make purchasing decisions based upon specific behaviors and risk tolerance. Purchasing takes place when perceived benefits are met or exceeded by the paid price. This philosophy applies whether you are buying a meal or a major piece of capital equipment.

Understanding that there are very different buying behaviors within a single target market is critical to understanding your opportunity:

- **Innovators** – These buyers are always driven to be the first to try new products or services. They are risk takers and will adopt "bleeding-edge" technology knowing that it will be more expensive and have more problems than if they waited. They will, for example, sign-on with technology companies to beta test new software or hardware prior to mainstream release.

  These buyers are first-in and are limited in number, representing roughly two and one-half percent of the available target market. So, if you are about to introduce a new first-to-market offering that has a total market size of 1,000 prospective buyers, you actually only have twenty five likely adopters that may allow you to secure early market validation.

- **Early Adopters** – Much like Innovators, these buyers represent those that purchase first-release offerings, also enduring the highest prices and problem incidence. They are visionaries who are driven by advancement. These are the people who will line up outside a local electronics store to purchase the first release of new software, a new game, television, personal computer, or phone. They will invest in the application of cutting-edge technologies in the quest to stay ahead and to be first.

Just behind "Innovators" in risk tolerance, these adopters represent roughly thirteen and one-half percent of the available market. Together these two groups align with the introduction stage in a product's life cycle.

- **Early Majority** – These buyers will only adopt offerings that have been vetted and successful for others at solving a specific problem or need. These buyers never hurry for first releases, but rather wait for revision two or three to make sure a product works and the problems are solved. They represent roughly thirty four percent of the available market and, due to their significant size and closeness to Early Adopters, they are the most sought after buyer. This group of buyers reflects strongly with the growth and early maturity stage in a product's life cycle.

- **Late Majority** – More conservative, but representing similar needs and thirty four percent of the available market, this group will not adopt until offerings have been well vetted and become established, "low risk" purchases. This group of buyers matches up strongly with the late growth and early decline stage in a product's life cycle.

For many years, when it came to adopting computer technology, there was a common theme – "you can't get fired for buying IBM®." IBM had pioneered computer technology and done an excellent job of instilling a level of security in the purchase process so that when new, higher-risk competition like Compaq®, Dell®, Gateway®, or Sony® arrived, IBM truly owned the late majority buyer because the company was perceived as the safe choice.

Successful businesses in this category have secured a strong, trusted brand position prior to this stage in the product's life cycle.

- **Laggards** – Representing the final sixteen percent of the available market, these buyers will only change their behavior when they have no choice, when they must adopt to maintain routine or normal activities. They may also purchase because the price has dropped to a point where there is no real risk. As technical evolution increases in speed, many offerings end up bypassing this segment altogether. Typically, this category is not a market segment that is sought, but rather harvested in the decline stage of a product's life cycle.

Innovators and early adopters together represent only sixteen percent of the available market. Depending on the buyer profile, the complexity of the product, and the need for new offerings, growth to the larger, more conservative adoption categories can be quick, long, or fail to occur at all.

The technology industry has seen many lags and failures in widespread adoption. Geoffrey Moore's book, <u>Crossing the Chasm</u>[6], is dedicated to understanding the timing, psychological, and behavioral issues associated with moving from innovators and early adopters to the larger and later market segments. This book is a "must read" for businesses bringing new technology to market.

Prospective buying behavior is critical to understand because it can significantly narrow your actual prospect pool, as well as sharpen your ability to reach prospects with the appropriate message. The more you understand a specific target buyer, the easier and more cost effective it becomes to reach them with your business development activities. If your actual prospect pool turns out to be too small, you can adjust accordingly.

I had a consulting client that had invented a great product for the transportation industry. His product was sound and, in tests, provided the promised benefits. Yet, because an innovator must adopt first, and because the number of total prospective fleets was very limited, he learned that, at best, he would have less than three prospective buyers. In actuality, he had none. Great ideas must match up with buyers that will adopt them.

Life Cycles
Whether you have a new opportunity or are maintaining an existing venture, understanding the life cycle position of your offering(s) is critical. All product and service offerings follow a traditional life cycle; the cycle's term var-

ies greatly by offering. A "product life cycle" defines the span of a product in the market, from when it is first adopted to when it is no longer purchased. From the adoption by innovators to the final adoption by laggards (if applicable), each

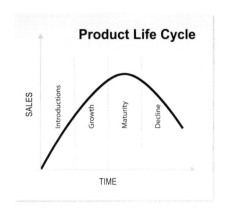

cycle stage comes with particular dynamics that will affect your ability to generate profitable revenue. Each stage provides unique opportunities and challenges, generates differing margins, and requires different marketing, selling and operational strategies and tactics.

The stages in a product life cycle:

Market introduction is characterized by high costs for both the product offering and market awareness. Initial buyers (in many cases) must be provided some level of adoption incentive. Sales volume is typically very low; there is little competition as many companies will simply wait to see how your product is accepted and then quickly jump into the market. (See innovator and early adopter stages previously discussed.)

Many potential competitors adopt a "we will not be first to market, but we will be best in the market over time" strategy. If the market rejects the new offering, they have not wasted time and money. This strategy does, however, allow new entrants to gain valuable market and brand equity if their new entry is quickly and publicly successful. This opportunity is a risk the more conservative providers run accordingly.

There are numerous stories of "spin-out" companies that were started by employees of larger businesses. These workers are typically those who had ideas for new developments that the company would not support. They took the risk and were successful, and in the process, created a formidable competitor for their previous employer.

The Growth Stage lines up with the emergence of the early adoption stage and represents a large portion of the early majority segment. In this stage, production costs are reduced as sales volume increases. Market awareness and profitability improves; pricing strategies to maximize market penetration are adopted. Competition begins to increase now that the market has validated the need; product differentiating improvements and variations are introduced. At this point, it is essential to be investing in new product offerings to prepare for the coming mature and decline stages.

The Mature Stage parallels the later portion of early majority adopters and continues to the start of the late majority segment. Product costs continue to fall as sales volume increases to maximum levels; development costs are amortized, and economies of scale are maximized. Market awareness reaches its maximum point, and competition expands to include even the most conservative entrants. Profit margins start to shrink as pricing starts to decline due to competitive pressures. Product differentiation becomes highly focused on features and benefits and the resulting price charged (value). At this juncture, it is critical to have introduced properly-aligned new market offerings.

The Decline Stage is supported by the late majority and laggard buyers. With this stage, costs have reached bottom. Sales volume continues to shrink, as does profitability. Competitors start to drop out of the market at the early part of this stage, leaving a smaller subset to close the cycle. This phase is typically supported by strong, stable competitors who have multiple, other offerings to offset operational expenses. Single entry competitors will be eliminated from the market in this stage if they have failed to add new products or to effectively evolve current offerings.

You can conduct significant research on life cycle trends and impact, but the point to be made here is that where your offering resides, or will reside on this cycle, is critical to understanding your opportunity, both short and long term. If you are early in the cycle, you will have less competition, more risk, a limited amount of available market, and a specific target behavior. If you are near the peak of the cycle, you will have a larger market along with the maximum amount of competition, and your ability to differentiate will be critical. If you are on the back side of the cycle, price will take over as a major differentiator; your ability to generate revenue and profit will become more difficult.

Businesses that traditionally perform well in the later stages of the cycle are those that have performed well and developed solid brand awareness and consumer support prior to this period. They have amortized development and tooling costs and can effectively lower pricing and maintain profitable margins.

Let us consider the VCR marketplace. Around the year 2000, the VCR peaked in its life cycle, and with the growth of DVD technology, sales began to decline. The number of competitors gradually dropped, as did the price over the next eight years to the point where today (2009), VHS tape production has stopped. If you can find a VCR, it can now be purchased for $50 (U.S.) or less. In many cases, the product includes an integrated DVD player because the traditional DVD format is now peaking; Blu-ray disk® technology is growing. When bandwidth allows the economical delivery of program content directly to the viewing device of your choice (TV, PC, iPod®, or phone), Blu-ray technology will also peak.

If you are an established provider and your product is peaking, will you stay in for the inevitable fall? Can you manage the downward price pressure and still make money? At what point should you abandon efforts to maintain market position without losing money? Do you have other offerings in earlier stages to ensure growth and vitality?

Many businesses become successful because customers just kept buying their product or service. The company never really understood why they purchased; only that they did. Suddenly sales started to drop drastically and they became confused. They hadn't changed anything, but sales dropped anyway. These businesses did not understand life cycle management. When a product declines in need, so does the need for their product, and these businesses perished, with management likely blaming the market or competition, in the process.

Successful, long-term businesses plan for each stage of both cycles. They understand the impact of the adoption and life cycles on their entire business model, constantly evolving, changing business development strategies, adding new offerings, and removing older offerings in an elegant and profitable manner.

RECIPE CHECK: STRATEGIC FIT

To validate the overall opportunity for your business, at a minimum, you should be able to answer the following questions:

- Who are the potential purchasers and how would you describe them?
  - Demographic – age, gender, race…
  - Psychographic – lifestyles, personalities, trends, genres…
  - Geographic – region, urban, rural, city, state, country…
  - Behavior – end use of the product, volume of use, brand loyalty, risk tolerance…

- How large is the overall market measured in dollars annually?
  - If a new category entrant, how many potential buyers can you reasonably assume will actually purchase the product/service on an annual basis and what will the growth trend be?
  - If similar offerings are already on the market, how big is the market now? Is it growing or shrinking? At what rate?
  - Where is the product in its life cycle and how will that impact you?

- How much of the market will adopt your product in place of others or in place of not adopting at all?
  - How do you differentiate?
  - Who cares and why?
  - Do not simply assume that you can garner a one percent share of market because the number sounds small and easily attainable.

Competition

Knowing your competition means being aware of what offerings they provide that do or will compete with yours. One must understand your competition price versus benefit position, or value position, as it relates to your own. You must identify their financial stability, as well as how their customers feel about their products or their brand strength. Knowing these details will help you accurately identify your "Strategic Fit" and continually tailor product offerings that will compete effectively.

There is no question that a level of educated estimating is necessary at this stage because, in most cases, all the desired data regarding your competition is not available. If you work hard at researching your competitors, the quality of estimating will far surpass guesswork.

First, do the research to understand what competition exists. Businesses get started, grow, and close on a regular basis without taking the time to really understand all of the competition. Sometimes, this occurs because they will not investigate, and sometimes, companies delude themselves into thinking they lack competitors, believing their product is so different or so much better than others that they simply do not compare.

Unless you are truly in an only provider position, you need to understand how you compare to alternatives that your buyers have (to buy nothing, to buy something else instead, etc.). If you are the sole provider and not generating competition, you might want to determine why. If you are the only provider today and your success is growing, you will have competition; it will be essential to track others accordingly. Remember, competition is not necessarily a bad thing. Competition validates the market need and, with increased business development efforts, helps your business generate demand.

A straight-forward exercise that you can do with your team is to plot the position of your business along with the competition on a "Fair Value Matrix" as shown. Measure benefits along the X axis and price along the Y axis. Now plot your relative position, along with

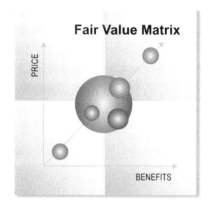

that of your competitors on this matrix. This will give you a visual representation of how you are positioned and the view your overall marketplace sees.

Critical to the success of this exercise is the use of quality data. When it comes to benefits, I *do not mean features*. Buyers pay for benefits, not features. Features are product attributes, like horsepower, number of channels, RPMs, color, size, and shape. Benefits are the meaningful outcomes produced by such attributes like speed, flexibility, durability, efficiency, and appearance. Many products have features that provide no benefit because the buyer does not need or want them. How many of you, remembering VCRs, had a need, or more importantly, the capability, to record twenty different shows over thirty days on twenty different channels? How many of you found it a benefit to turn on your television so you could read the menu of the VCR when programming?

When you compare your product to the competition, be very careful to look from a buyer's perspective and only compare benefits people will buy. Do not move yourself further to the right if you have additional features that buyers do not want, or worse yet, see as a distraction. Be aware that it is possible to add features that actually reduce the benefit of your offerings.

When plotting your position, and that of the competition, you can use different sizes of circles to indicate the relative size of each competitor as shown. When complete, you should have a good view of your relative competitive position in the market. Now, the questions to answer are:

- Does your position match what you thought it was?
- Is your position where you want to be?
- Can you be successful in this position?

If you are one of the smaller circles inside or overlapping the major competitor (big circle), should you be re-thinking your position? Is there an opportunity in the gap between the competitive center and the lone provider in the upper right? Be aware that just because there is a hole in the matrix does not mean there is a viable position to be filled. You need to conduct research to make the right determination.

It is important to note that competition will likely live along the forty-five degree line, as shown. Having a higher price with lower benefits will attract few buyers. Having the lowest price and the most benefits will likely not produce effective profit margins, with the clear exception of new technological advancements and / or the introduction of disruptive new technology.

In the case of advancing technology, the lower right quadrant will gradually become the new matrix with quadrants of its own. The key for your business, if faced with this trend, is not to get caught lagging in the old matrix. If you are the first business driving this shift, you may have specific marketing and adoption challenges. If you are the last to leave, you may not survive.

When it comes to competition, you should understand:
- Current, competing products and how they compare
- New products in development and how they will compare
- Brand strength and time in the market
- Size and relative financial strength
- Methods of distribution
- Marketing communication strategies
- Geographic coverage

Differentiating from your competition is critical to your continued success. Also significant is the ability to defend that distinction. You can protect your position by continually creating new products that are ahead of the competition. Many that pursue this method accept that their products will be copied by competition, and in many cases see that as helpful. They are masters of product development and the copying by competitors simply validates their brand. This is a development-intensive strategy and one that must be employed carefully; it is most easily employed by businesses with a developed brand.

Businesses can also guard their position by simply executing better than everyone else. They may sell the same products as their competition, but they simply execute in a better manner, thereby securing and retaining loyal customers. In this case, they let competitors focus on product development, and once complete, they simply do it better. Think of the businesses you patronize just because you would rather purchase from them, not because they are the only ones with the product. Differentiating due to execution excellence must be validated by customers, not just perceived internally.

Also critical to differentiation are the legal forms of protecting what a company identifies as its intellectual property (IP). Patents are commonly the first type of security considered. Many believe that a patent is a sure predictor of success. Many believe that once you get a patent, the hard work is done. Without addressing this subject in depth, I will say this about patents:

- Patents with meaningful and broad coverage are getting harder and harder to obtain. The sheer number of patents already awarded, as well as the active case load for examiners, significantly impacts both the ability to get meaningful coverage, as well as the time it takes to get any coverage at all. On average, it now takes two to four years for a patent to be issued – domestic or foreign. Many, by the time they are awarded, are very limited in scope and protection.

- Securing a U.S. Patent now requires an investment of between $10,000 and $30,000, with complex technologies sometimes costing considerably more. Foreign patents have similar costs and escalate as the countries covered increase. Patents also require ongoing maintenance and defense, which can add significantly to the investment over time.

- Patents provide the ability for you to exclude others from doing specifically what your awarded claims recite. This protection requires that you take appropriate action, possibly including expensive and protracted litigation.

- Patents can be "worked around." Once they are awarded, they are a matter of public record, and so is the complete description of how your product is made.

- Patents are awarded to the actual inventor(s) of the idea.

They cannot be issued in the name of a company. You cannot choose to put them in one person's name if more individuals were involved in the design process. They must be filed and issued in the names of all who contributed to the conception of the invention. Once awarded, they belong to each and every person named on the patent individually, unless such rights are otherwise contractually assigned.

- Patents can be one piece of your IP strategy, but they should not be your only strategy.

I have multiple patents issued in my name, and I have helped many others with the process. Patents provide legal rights and provide marketing leverage; in some cases, they offer strong competitive positioning. Before proceeding, get good legal advice from patent counsel who specialize in your area of business and have strong references.

Along with, or aside from, patents, you should also include trademarks, copyrights, trade secrets, and legal agreements in your IP strategy.

Trademarks can become the strongest piece of IP you own, and unlike patents, which have a twenty-year life, trademarks can be protected forever. A strong trademark and the brand associated with that mark have created very successful businesses over time. 3M®'s Post-it® Brand Notes is a clear example. By the time 3M truly engaged in the protection of its now famous sticky notes, it was too late to file a patent. Instead, the IP team at 3M filed a trademark application for sticky notes in the color canary yellow. The marketing team then went about building the demand for Post-it Brand Notes – in canary yellow.[7] To this day, although there are multiple other color and brand choices now available, canary yellow Post-it Brand Notes are the number one selling brand. Your brand and trademark can be yours for life if properly managed, and they arguably provide the strongest form of IP available.

A few notes on trademarks:

- Trademarks (^{TM}) may be used for products and service marks (^{SM}) may be used for services. The TM and SM designations may be applied by the creating business / person with no legal filing action required. The use of the SM or TM simply indicates that the business considers that mark to be their property.

- To secure additional specific legal rights to your mark, an appropriate filing to the United States Patent and Trademark Office (USPTO) or other global entity must be submitted. Like patents, the trademark process can be lengthy but is generally less expensive. Plan on one to three years to receive a ® registered trademark (service mark), and like patents, expect multiple challenges from the trademark examiner regarding competitive and previous marks. I spent nearly five years securing a single trademark, so have patience.

- In the U.S., you can save time when creating a trademark by doing initial research on your own. Go to the U.S. Patent and Trademark Office website (http://www.uspto.gov); search both patents and trademarks to get an initial analysis of your ability to secure protection. A more thorough search by a qualified legal representative is strongly recommended prior to an actual filing.

Copyright law has evolved to automatically protect the creator or author of original written materials. The right to such written creations resides with the author alone, unless otherwise statutorily assigned (work made for hire), or contractually assigned. Filing and securing formal copyright protection can be done by the author, or the employer, in the case of assignment. If awarded, additional damages protection may be available in litigation if certain legal requirements are met.

Trade secrets are formulas, recipes, and processes that you consider to be secret and under no circumstances will be revealed. For example, consider the recipes for Coke® or Kentucky Fried Chicken / KFC®. In both cases, the formula is considered a trade secret by the company and protected accordingly, providing specific legal rights if the secret is stolen or otherwise unintentionally revealed.

Contracts and agreements are critical in the IP process when it comes to the company wanting to own IP created by its employees. As mentioned before, patents, and sometimes copyrights, are the property of the author of the material. Just because ideas, designs and materials were created by your employee does not mean you have all legal right to the IP. A non-officer employee can simply sell his or her patent rights to the highest bidder; they can also give them away, or go to work for your competitor and share the rights. They can do all these things, unless you have a legal agreement to the contrary.

Most businesses have employees sign agreements upon employment that specifically assign, to the company, all rights to the IP created by that employee while employed by the company. In this case, the employee's name still resides on the patents, but the company maintains full legal control. Keep this in mind when working with outside contractors as well. For example, if you are working with an advertising agency to create your logo, your product names, copy for your literature, etc., the IP surrounding those items resides with the agency that created it. This holds true for software, hardware or any other copyrightable material created by outside contractors.

When it comes to protecting your position in the market, understanding and protecting your IP is of critical importance. Get qualified legal advice, as I did for this discussion.[8]

RECIPE CHECK: STRATEGIC FIT

When it comes to competition, at a minimum, you should be able to answer the following questions:

- Who is the competition?
  - How do your current products compare on a fair value matrix?
  - What new products are they introducing and how will you compare?
  - How big and strong are they financially?
  - What is the strength of their brand in the market?
  - What is their distribution or sales strategy?
  - What is their marketing communications strategy?
  - How do they support their customers?

- How will you protect your position?
  - Constant development and first to market
  - Better execution
  - Intellectual property protection

If you cannot answer the "Recipe Check" questions provided to this point for a business that you are starting or one you already operate, you cannot aim your business effectively. Highly successful businesses, especially ones that are rewarded over time, strategically direct their businesses by using this type of information.

Can You Provide the Offering Identified?

If you have successfully completed the first part of your "Strategic Fit" analysis, you have identified or validated:

- A product or service for which there is a clear need
- A definable audience
- An ability to differentiate and compete

The next question is can you actually produce the product you have defined? Everyone knows that there is a clear need for a cure for cancer. There is a very identifiable market with adequate volumes and a great intensity of need. However, the ability to actually create the desired product continues to elude us. Identifying a valid need does not always identify a product or service that can actually be delivered.

Many products fail because they simply cannot be produced and delivered as required to satisfy the identified needs. A company may have four specific benefits that their product must have to compete effectively. In the design or manufacturing process, they determine that they can only fulfill three of the four requirements, and since they are ready to go to market, they proceed. The end-product delivered is something less than *promised or required*, and the business suffers accordingly.

On the other hand, businesses that start with the product and go in search of a market either modify the actual need identified to fit, or they make unrealistic promises as to what the product can and will deliver (known as "pretty baby syndrome"). Ultimately, they provide a product that no one really wants – a product that cannot differentiate from competitive offerings or one that creates customer dissatisfaction and damage to their brand. There are an untold number of stories where businesses made the necessary promise to a market or individual customer to "get the order," only to fail in delivery.

Businesses fail daily because they lose sight of what they *can do* in relation to what the *customers want*. There is a clear balance between satisfying customer and company needs, and when you sacrifice either for the other, your "Recipe" is diminished.

RECIPE CHECK: STRATEGIC FIT

Make sure you provide the product for which the need was identified:
- Deliver the benefits required by the customer without adding unnecessary complexity.
- Do not make claims for which you cannot deliver.

Can You Make Money?

So perhaps now you have learned that there is a viable need and a feasible market for a product you can produce or already are producing. What is next? Many go forward at this point without truly understanding if they actually have a profitable product, one that will earn their business a profitable margin while meeting the price points necessary to generate sales.

I have seen many businesses that are unprofitable because management never identified the real cost to produce and deliver their products, or because they never identified the price point(s) needed to position their product(s) to generate the needed revenue. *Be aware that your price also represents your brand, and selecting a price point is about more than margin. (More about this later under marketing strategies.)*

When trying to understand the cost of producing your product, or the cost of goods sold (known as COGS – labor and material content per unit produced), collect good information and analyze it well. If you are already in business, make sure that you look at the actual cost to produce, deliver and support every product on a regular basis. Many companies have individual products that are actually losing money on every sale because they do not calculate and review such expenses and are simply unaware of the impact on their financial performance.

In one of my previous career roles, while examining one of our key products, I learned it would have been more profitable to simply give each customer who ordered that item from us a check for $200 to buy a competitor's product. We were losing a minimum of $500 on every unit sold because of serious service and warranty issues. We were also damaging our brand in the process. This sounds unbelievable, but the losses, until researched, were simply hidden in a rolled-up overhead.

In other cases, producers believe that they have to conduct some business at a loss to earn the more profitable business or to simply keep the factory running to absorb overhead. "We can make it up in volume" is an all-too-common phrase in the manufacturing world. While there is certainly a volume and cost relationship to manufacturing, there is also a cost for inventory, capital employed, obsolete and scrap, etc. My philosophy is, if you do not make money on a sale, don't make the sale. If you cannot sell what you have at a profit, you have not identified a viable business model.

When initially introducing new products, many short-run volumes and higher unit costs are tolerated to test market acceptance. If this is your strategy, make sure you understand what the predicted or forecasted volume costs will be before the testing begins so that you can later make a profit at the selling price. Remember that market testing is about more than the product itself, and do not believe that profitability always comes with volume. Most importantly, do not project volumes you can never attain just to make planned margins effective.

If you are introducing a new product, spend the money to get necessary documentation for good cost projections at realistic volumes. If you are introducing a product that will be sold through a third party one-step (dealer or reseller) or two-step (distributor and dealer) distribution model, understand the discounts, commissions, and independent representative fees associated. In many situations, you will need a retail price point as high as five to seven times your COGS to attract distribution and make money in the process.

RECIPE CHECK: STRATEGIC FIT

To determine the viability of your product/service profitability, at a minimum, you should understand:

- The strategic price point that will properly position your product and cause the desired amount of revenue.
- Any distribution margin requirements, i.e. dealer or distributor discounts. What will be your net sales price?
- What does it actually cost to produce your product (COGS)?
- How much is left? (Gross margin). If you don't have enough money left over to cover the balance of your expenses and to still make a profit, you have a problem.

THE RIGHT INGREDIENTS

If you perform the above exercise for your product(s), you can quickly determine if you have a financially viable model. Many times there are products for which there is a clear need in the market, but at the same time companies simply cannot make money at the price customers are willing to pay. Unfortunately, many such items get to market without management understanding the situation, wounding or killing the company in the process. Do the math and make a good decision. Profitability comes from a solid pricing strategy designed around a clearly identified "Strategic Fit."

Can You Consistently Deliver?
There is a need for your offering; you can differentiate. You know who and how big your market is. You can produce the offering and also make money. Before you hit execute, you must also determine if you have the ability to deliver on a consistent basis and support the offering you have identified. Can you really build and deliver on time, on quantity, and on quality?

It is clearly possible to identify everything we have discussed to date and be unable to deliver the product on time, quantity, or quality because you failed to properly project adoption rates and assemble the production capabilities needed to deliver.

You may remember a television advertisement during the dot-com boom where a web-based start-up company launched their new website. Presumably the entire company (all three of them) were huddled around the monitor waiting for orders to hit. First, there were a few orders and they cheered. Then there were hundreds of orders, and they cheered. Then there were thousands of orders, and they were silent. Then there were hundreds of thousands of orders, and they were out of business, before they ever really started.

In December of 1996 AOL® dropped its internet access price from a pay-for-use model to a $19.95 per month, unlimited usage program.[9] The goal was to drive up new customer acquisition and an ad campaign was launched accordingly. Consumer acceptance was immediate; so many new and existing users subscribed that their available bandwidth was exceeded. AOL's network was not prepared to handle a nearly 3X jump in bandwidth requirement, so its customers, both new and old, simply could not get the service for which they subscribed. What followed were significant investments by AOL in technology, public relations, and defense of class-action lawsuits. AOL clearly recovered, but learned a very important lesson about understanding the impact of price points on market demand and the ensuing ability to provide the product promised.

RECIPE CHECK: STRATEGIC FIT

Not being able to consistently deliver your product, as it was purchased, in a timely manner can seriously damage your business. You should know:

- How will you provide the quantity of product required on a consistent basis?
- How will you react to sudden increases or decreases in demand?
- Can you react without adding unnecessary fixed overhead?
- Can you support increasing volumes after initial delivery?
- Have you planned for configuration or revision controls?

Will the Environment Support Your Business?

There are many market influences that can and will impact your business over time. Most will be those over which you have no control but will have great power over your ability to succeed. They are, perhaps, easiest to remember as the acronym "STEEP," featured in the book <u>Beyond Strategic Vision</u> by Michael Cowley and Ellen Domb.[10]

There are five influential factors:

- **Social factors** – how is society evolving and how will that impact your business? Are there social groups you should be watching that will be future prospects? Will your current customers be affected?
- **Technological factors** – how is technology evolving and how will that impact your business? How will new technology affect the components or overall production of your product? How will it affect your inventory or the life cycle of your product? Will it open opportunities for new products?
- **Economic factors** – how is the economy evolving and how will that impact your business? How will recession or inflation impact your business? How will changes in healthcare expense affect you? How will the value of your national currency affect you?
- **Environmental factors** – how is the environment evolving and how will that impact your business? Will you offer "green" product alternatives? Will you incorporate "green" building and manufacturing processes? Will changing weather patterns (rainfall, temperature, etc.) impact your business?
- **Political factors** – how are local, regional, national, and world politics evolving and how will that impact your

business? How will pending and future legislation impact your business? Will a nationalized healthcare program impact your business? How will evolving tax structures impact your business?

Recessions, wars, elections, legislation, evolution, education, development, weather, and the effects of human behavior will all impact your business over time. For example, if you are in the military defense industry, a nation or world at conflict is a political factor that can help you succeed. If you are an alternative energy provider, the price of oil will have a great influence on your business. If your product produces significant greenhouse gases, the focus on the environment, and related legislation, may impact your success.

In all such cases, influences out of your control will affect your ability to succeed, both positively and negatively, and these forces must be understood, projected, and planned for accordingly. Businesses that fail and blame one or more of the influences listed as "bad luck" could possibly have avoided such failure by understanding and reacting to the projected impact in advance. When unknowing businesses reap the benefit of positive influences, some call it "good luck" as well. If you research and plan accordingly, less of your success will depend on luck. Ignorance is not a viable excuse for failure, nor should good luck be deemed good planning. Understand what influences your business, and use it to your advantage.

RECIPE CHECK: STRATEGIC FIT

Understanding the overall market environment in which you are and will be doing business is critical to your success.

- Will you put a plan in place to regularly review updated information on Social, Technological, Economic, Environmental, and Political (STEEP) changes in the market?
- Will you assign the job of monitoring these influencers to specific team members?
- Will you make timely adjustments to your plan based upon the knowledge gained?

Do You Have a Strategic Fit?

Identifying your "Strategic Fit" based upon quality information will significantly increase your chance of success, whether you are trying to grow an existing business or to create a new one. A proper "Fit" analysis will allow you to identify and to profitably defend a valid product / market position. At a minimum this will require:

- **Valid Need** - An identifiable and valid market need that can justify the entry or ongoing adoption of your product.
- **Valid Opportunity** - Focused and identifiable target market(s) that you can reach and who will buy enough of your product or service over a predictable period of time. You must be able to differentiate and defend your position accordingly.
- **Valid Product** - The ability to provide the identified and required benefits as needed to induce adoption and differentiate from competition.
- **Valid Pricing** - Price points the target market(s) will actually pay, that will support the brand position, and

allow your business the margins necessary for viability and growth.

- **Valid Operation** - The overall ability of your company to consistently deliver and support your product or service, while meeting growth projections.
- **Valid Environment** - A market environment and related influences that support acceptance or continued position, as well as the growth of your product, over time.

If you answer all these questions objectively, you will be able to determine whether or not you have a product/service that has a viable place in the market, whether you are a new business or have been in business for over a century. Be honest and remember if you cannot accurately and factually define a "Fit," your success, or continued success will be based upon chance.

If you have a "Strategic Fit", then it's time to write a good business plan. The good news is that once you have completed this exercise you will have compiled the content needed to complete the "Strategic Fit" section of your business plan.

SCORE YOUR BUSINESS

At this point – take a moment and score your business on page 185. If you can truly identify your "Fit" based upon all the components discussed in this chapter, score yourself at ten. If you can identify some of the components but still need to work on others, score yourself accordingly. If you simply cannot identify your "Fit" at all, other than with a gut feeling or because you have always had customers but do not know why, the honest score would be zero. As we go through the chapters, scoring will allow you to identify opportunities for improved performance, so grade yourself honestly. After all, only you will see the results, if that is what you choose.

In the Supplement you will find web access to a complete outline for the "Strategic Fit" section. This guide will help you through the needed information and provide a proper format to include in your business plan.

BUSINESS PLAN
A Written Guide to Your Success

In the previous chapter, we identified the viable reason(s) *why* your business is, or can be, successful. The next step is to create the plan that will outline *how* you can realize and sustain ongoing success.

Most business owners or executives come to work, open the door, and become consumed by the day. Meetings, phone calls, e-mails, and people walking through their door dictate priorities. There may have been the intention to work on other things, maybe even planning, but more important things needed immediate attention "today." Closing time arrives and they leave, tired from another "hard day at the office." In this cycle, day after day, businesses are pulled in unknown and unplanned directions because management spends its days working "in" the business, instead of "on" the business.

Very few people start a trip without a roadmap and destination in mind. Yet, every day around the globe, businesses are driven with no clear plan or destination. If you do not plan where your business is going and how it is going to get there, market forces will do the planning for you. This process might provide adequate results, but for most companies, this lack of proactive direction compromises focus and profitability.

Whether you are creating a new business or accelerating an existing one, a business plan is absolutely essential to success. This document provides the strategic and tactical foundation of a strong, defendable business. Very few businesses, if any, succeed routinely based upon simple reaction to daily needs.

You can be a "one-hit wonder" and be wildly successful by luck or by making some good decisions at the right points in time. When outside influences like competition, technology change, a sagging economy, or an evolving market demand cause unexpected change, you will wish you had done a better job of planning. As the old saying goes, "failing to plan is planning to fail." If you are running a business without a plan, it is likely that your business will fail for reasons that could, and should have, been planned around.

Business plans are not documents you write once to get a loan or equity capital, only to be stored prominently on a shelf, never to be looked at again. Business plans are road-maps to success that outline: (1) what you are going to do; (2) why you are doing it; (3) who is going to do it; (4) when it is going to be done; (5) how much it will cost to do it; (6) and what you will gain in the end. Plans provide guidance to you and your team; they provide accountability, a sense of security, and a way to measure performance against intent. From establishing your mission, to investing the generated profits, your plan will be a reflection of your business' capability to succeed.

Think of a business plan as the foundation element of a successful business and build the strongest foundation you can. If you produce a great plan for the success of your business, that plan will work equally well for raising the needed capital for its execution. *Do not write plans to raise money, write plans to make money! Plans that make money will attract money!*

Live It

Planning is an ongoing process, and if done right, becomes a part of your daily business life. All parts of your plan are dynamic because the market is constantly changing. If you and your team live your plan by writing, executing, monitoring, and modifying it as needed, your business will show the results.

Make it Readable

A plan should read like a good "how-to" book. The executive summary should convince someone to read the balance of the plan. The flow should be logical, feature complete facts, and have an overall intent that is clearly understandable. As a fund manager and a veteran of many business plans, I can tell you that those written using the "1.1.3" model templates can be very disjointed, difficult to read, and ultimately worthless. Business planning is not a fill-in-the-blank process; planning cannot be effectively accomplished by simply answering specific questions in different ways. *Plans must tell your story.*

If you Google® "business plans," you will find over fifty million possible resources, ideas, outlines, and opinions – some written by experts who actually have experience creating and executing plans and many by academics and theorists. As a student of planning, with significant first-hand experience at both business creation and existing business acceleration, what follows is an outline that I have found to be very effective.

I was fortunate in my early business years to find an experienced business plan mentor. My father, who was Vice President and Publisher, Better Homes and Gardens Books® (BH&G®), introduced me to the executive in charge of planning at Meredith® Corporation (BH&G's parent). From its' founding in 1902, Meredith had grown consistently for decades and continues its growth today, with a strong planning discipline. From this person, I also developed a strong discipline that has served me well in my career. Although I modified items over time, much of what he taught me is incorporated in the outline below. Feel free to modify the list as your business dictates but remember that all the components indicated are critical to success.

The remaining sections of this chapter will outline the content for each component:
- The Executive Summary
- Things We Have Learned
- Function and Scope
- Mission and Principles
- Strategic Fit (Situation Analysis)
- Assumptions and Critical Issues
- Strengths and Weaknesses
- Objectives and Goals
- Strategies and Tactics
- Operations Plan
- Resources and Financials
- Monitoring Plan
- Action Plan

Executive Summary
Many "experts" suggest writing the executive summary last. If you draft the executive summary first, the content will serve as the framework for the rest of your business plan. If you cannot create a compelling summary, then there is no need to write the rest of the plan.

Your executive summary should be concise, compelling,

and include the following:

- Who are you? What do you do?
  - What is the product/service?
  - What does it do?
  - What benefits does it provide?

- Who is your market?
  - Descriptions of your target market(s)
  - Types of businesses or users
  - Size of the annual total market opportunity (current and projected)
  - Geographic scope of the market (local, state, regional, national, global)

- Why will you be successful?
  - Explain the compelling reason(s) why the market needs your product or service
  - How does it compare to the competition?
  - How will you defend your product? Do you have patents that protect your property? Will you be the first to market?

- How will you execute?
  - How will you produce your product?
  - How will you price, advertise, promote and generate interest in your product?
  - How will you sell and support your product – internet, direct reps, dealers, distributors, etc.

- Who will execute?
  - What is the organizational structure?

- Who is the leadership team? Include short profiles of each team member to validate his or her areas of expertise. Not everyone on the team has to be internal; however, you should demonstrate competency in marketing, sales, product development, operations, IT, and finance.

- What results will you achieve over the next three years?
  - Projected sales in each year
  - Projected earnings in each year

Be sure your executive summary is quantifiable. The claims you make must be able to stand up to an inquisition, without you in the room to defend it. Predictions must match up and be supported by the details of the plan. If you are raising money, remember that bankers and investors are interested in viable businesses; they do not get caught up in what's cool, unless it's profitable. Above all, make sure your executive summary reads like the jacket on a good novel. Tell the story in a way that makes sense, has validity, and sells your plan.

Things We Have Learned
This element is something you will not find in other plan outlines, but something I have added over the years to make sure my businesses paid attention to what we were learning as we were learning. Make a simple list of the things you "learned" in the previous year that were new, unexpected, or unplanned. Possible scenarios include: (1) your competitor reacted in a way you did not anticipate; (2) the economy impacted your business in an unexpected way; (3) your target market needs changed in a manner you did not anticipate; (4) or any other "lesson" you learned. Continually list these

items in your plan, adding to them in pencil or ink as the current year progresses; you are then much more likely to pay attention to the related impacts going forward.

Function and Scope

"Function" describes who you are, what you do, and who you do it for. "Scope" describes where you perform. For example, *we are the leading manufacturer of "xyz" products for the "xyz" global market, or, we are North America's leading provider of "xyz" services in the xyz industry.* This description will range from one paragraph to one page, depending on the number of product offerings and markets covered. Out of this section, you should be able to craft a clear "elevator pitch," so that the next time someone says, "What do you do," you do not fumble with a long explanation. I am amazed by the number of business executives, as well as their employees, who cannot quickly deliver a concise answer to that question.

The number one "ice breaking" question at any networking opportunity is, *"what do you do?"* Every time someone asks, you have the opportunity to look professional and create an important contact. If you knew that the person asking had the ability to significantly improve your business life, would you care more how you would answer? Have you ever asked that question only to get a complete barrage of information in which you were not the least bit interested? Treat everyone with the same respect when that question is asked and practice a concise answer. "I am (insert title) for (insert company name). We are the world's leading supplier of XYZ widgets to the computer industry." Or "I am (insert title) for (insert company name), and we provide market leading XYZ services to the insurance industry on a global basis."

Some of the best business opportunities of your lifetime will present themselves in networking situations. In airports, on a plane, at social gatherings or conventions you will ask or be asked that question. If you polish the answer and teach your team so that they are also prepared, your business opportunities will improve accordingly.

Mission

Your "mission" defines who you are and where you want to go. It embodies the culture of your business as well as a long-term destination. It provides focus for your internal team, a foundation for the overall brand image your business is taking to market, and it is measureable and attainable. In one sentence to one paragraph, your mission statement will guide overall decision making and serve as the fundamental gauge by which all business results are measured. Your mission must differentiate you from others and be something in which you and your employees believe and to which you aspire.

Examples:

Sony® _(early 1950's): "Our mission is to become the company most known for changing the worldwide poor-quality image of Japanese products."_

Wal-Mart® _"Our mission is to give ordinary folk the chance to buy the same thing as rich people."_[11]

Everyone would agree that each of those mission statements accurately fits the brand impression now generated by the company's name that created the statement. Decide where you want to go and how you want to be seen; write it down, and make it happen.

Principles

The principles of your business are statements that define the core values, ethics and overall characteristics guiding action toward your employees, customers, community and yourself. Principles clarify how you will be accountable to your customers, what they can expect from you, and why they should believe you will deliver on your promise. Principles should inspire support and commitment, be easy to understand, and simple to repeat. They should address your employees and resonate with other stakeholders in your business (partners, suppliers, investors, etc.).

The principles of your business should encompass the critical operational and ethical components that you will never compromise for any reason — especially if you are the boss. The ability to create principles and live by them at all times will create a strong culture in and for your business. The culture will then determine the effort and dedication you will get from your team. Your ability to reach or exceed goals will rely heavily, if not completely, on the right company culture.

Listed below are the principles I have and continue to employ. I gathered the core of these principles from the Meredith Corporation (See supplement) decades ago and modified them to fit my business needs. There are no extra points for creativity or being original in this area. Your job is to establish and live by principles that will build the kind of culture needed to accomplish your mission. Feel free to use the ones below for your business, if you so choose.

• *Our primary focus is personal and corporate success over the long term.*

- *Customers are our company's lifeblood. We are dedicated to building enduring relationships with them by understanding their needs and meeting or exceeding their expectations with high-quality, high-value products and services.*
- *Our employees are the company's most important resources. We expect integrity, creativity, initiative, teamwork, respect and individual judgment. We encourage an entrepreneurial style. We value and reward excellent achievement. We believe that work enjoyment and company performance are closely related.*
- *We treasure the good reputation of our company, its products and services, and its people. Our reputation matters in everything we do.*
- *We believe that good citizenship requires concern for the community in which we operate and we encourage corporate and employee participation.*

The company mission statement and principles should be framed and posted in a common place for all employees to review and rely upon in their day-to-day decision making. They should be available for visiting customers to read and, most importantly, to witness. All company decisions must be founded on the mission and principles.

Strategic Fit Analysis:
Insert the work from your "Strategic Fit" analysis.

Critical Issues and Assumptions:
Every successful business needs to make assumptions and identify critical issues needed to be successful. Without getting too broad, make a list of the situations and critical is-

sues which you assume will or will not take place. These are things that are foundational to your business reaching its goals. This list should be monitored, so that in the event one or more of the items are compromised, your business can take immediate action.

For each item on the list, you should spend time thinking about what your contingency plan would be so that you can act immediately. For every sample here, think about how it might affect your business if the opposite event happened.

Some typical assumptions and critical issues may include:

The company:
- We will be able to attract and retain the required staff.
- Our suppliers will be able to deliver on time.
- Our production operation will be adequate to meet up to 130% of projected demand.
- We will be able to secure the lending instruments needed to cash flow our business growth.

The product:
- We will secure the necessary regulatory approvals and certifications.
- The product will perform as planned.
- We will be able to produce the product at predicted costs.

The industry:
- The competition will not significantly reduce its pricing in reaction to our new offering.
- No new entrants will leapfrog our technology with a new offering.
- Oil will stay above $75.00 per barrel (When I wrote the first draft of this page, oil was over $140.00 per barrel.

Less than a year later is was below $40.00 a barrel. Think of the businesses impacted by that variance.)

The country:
- There will be no attacks on United States soil.
- The prime lending rate will not exceed seven percent.
- Healthcare will remain in the private sector.

If you make a quality list and identify contingency plans accordingly, your business will be less volatile. Prior to September 11, 2001, few businesses had a contingency plan for hostile actions on American soil; many do now. Companies were terribly impacted by the ultimate economic impact and have put plans in place for the future. Spend time on this list; content and contingent planning will make a significant difference at a critical time.

Strengths and Weaknesses
A traditional SWOT analysis ("Strengths, Weaknesses, Opportunities, and Threats", coined by Albert S. Humphrey)[12] is a great exercise and can be included here, if desired. Strengths and weaknesses are internal impacts on your business; opportunities and threats deal with impacts from outside your business. Outside impacts relating to opportunities and threats were noted in the "Strategic Fit" analysis. As a result, the strengths and weaknesses' component is all that is necessary at this point in the plan, but you can certainly do all four categories if so desired.

Make a list of your business' strengths as they specifically relate to accomplishing your mission; make a similar list of the weaknesses with the same purpose. It is critical that you are honest and identify both lists in a quality manner. Some typical examples might include:

Company Strengths:
- Strong established brand
- Quality, established distribution channel
- Strong financial position; able to finance growth internally

Product Strengths:
- Strong patent and trademark protection
- Technical functionality superior to competition
- COGS lower than competition for competitive products

Company Weaknesses:
- Inability to attract key talent needed for growth
- Poor financial position – unable to finance needed growth
- New market entry; no brand established yet

Product Weaknesses:
- No intellectual property protection
- Technical functionality problems continue to plague the product(s)
- COGS higher than competitive products due to lower volumes or out-of-date manufacturing processes

Between this list, your "Strategic Fit" analysis, and the assumptions and critical issues list, you should have identified all the potential impacts, weak areas, and strengths of your business model. This analysis will allow you to focus on improving the vulnerabilities to quickly react in the event of unplanned events, and to leverage your strengths to accomplish your plan.

RECIPE CHECK: BUSINESS PLAN

Before you set specific goals and objectives, make sure you have assembled the information needed to establish a foundation for your business success.

- Have you established your company's mission and written the principles needed to establish the culture required?
- Have you written a compelling executive summary?
- Have you established your "Strategic Fit" and identified the assumptions and critical issues that must be monitored?
- Do you understand your business strengths and weaknesses as they relate to your ability to succeed?

Objectives and Goals

At this point in the process, you have validated a defendable "*Fit*" in the market, established a clear mission with strong principles, identified assumptions and critical issues and outlined your strengths and weaknesses. Now, you are in a position to establish realistic goals. For the purpose of this book, I am going to simply use the terms "Goals and Objectives" interchangeably to define outcomes that can be specifically measured in time and performance.

A clear statement of goals is crucial to the core success of your business. Goals are key when planning strategic activities and formulating your business processes. Setting goals gives your management team a benchmark providing direction for aligning actions and efforts, and aiding in the evaluation of performance.

Goals should be SMART – Specific, Measurable, Attainable, Relevant and Timely.[13] Specific goals are precise and should identify the desired outcome in a way that is easily understood. For example, "We will grow sales." This statement is not specific. "We will grow sales of iPod® Nanos" is more specific. "We will grow sales of the 16G iPod Nanos" is better. "We will grow sales of 16G iPod Nanos in the Hispanic market" is even better still. Yet none of these statements are measurable.

Measurable goals are phrased so that progress toward achievement can be monitored; you will then know with certainty whether or not goals have been met. For example, "We will grow sales of 16G iPod Nanos in the Hispanic Market by 10%" is measurable, but by what date? Goals must also be measurable in time. For the final example, I offer, "We will grow sales of 16G iPod Nanos in the Hispanic Market by 10% by 2010."

Goals must be attainable. They should not be so easy that achieving them will come with little or no effort. You should not formulate goals that you have no chance of accomplishing. Your entire team will understand impossible goals as not attainable; motivation and morale will be impacted, especially if incentive compensation is involved. Goals must be realistic.

Goals must be relevant to, and focused on, attaining the overall corporate mission. Those that are not focused confuse your team and derail your efforts. For example, many times cost-cutting goals run afoul of product quality goals. Constantly taking cost out of a product while at the same time maintaining or raising quality level requirements can easily become a conflicting and frustrating situation. Make sure your goals are aligned and that you have company-wide buy-in. Forcing competing or unattainable goals upon your employees is an ideal way to kill morale, create a negative culture and start down the path to liquidation.

Goals must also be timely and must relate to business at hand. Setting goals far into the future with no basis for attainment provides no tangible traction from your team. Your mission is your long-term success measure; make sure your plan goals are contained and timely to the actions and accomplishments you can substantiate.

Typical annual goals include:
- Profit and loss (P&L) goals (*revenue, COGS, gross margin, expenses, etc.*)
- Balance sheet and net cash flow goals
- Revenue and net profit per employee goals
- Product development goals
- Market share goals
- Efficiency goals
- Personnel goals, etc…

RECIPE CHECK: BUSINESS PLAN

When setting goals:
- Make sure they are specific, measurable, attainable, relevant and timely
- Make sure they motivate and stretch your team, but make sure they are feasible
- Make sure all your goals are focused on the same end, attaining your mission; do not create conflicting goals

Strategies and Tactics

At this point in the plan you are hopefully starting to see that there is a building process underway. Now that you have identified your "Fit," your mission, your principles, your assumptions and critical issues, your strengths and weaknesses, you can now start identifying the strategies and tactics needed to attain the established goals and objectives.

Most businesses, new or old, want to skip this prior work phase and start the planning process right here. If you skipped to this section, ignoring beginning elements, you are missing the point. Strategies and tactics outline what you are going to do to attain your goals and objectives, and a long-term mission. It is impossible to establish great strategies and tactics without all the information you have gathered in the "Strategic Fit" and business plan chapters. The better the information; the better your strategies. The more front-end work you skip; the more guessing you will need to do. Consequently, the lower your chance of success will become, and the greater the possibility of catastrophic results.

As an analogy, General George S. Patton is lauded as being the most effective wartime general in United States military history for his service before and during World War II. Patton reigned victorious over his enemy because he was a student of military history, his enemy, the country, the terrain, and even the weather. George C. Scott's famous line in the movie Patton, when his namesake was to fight Erwin Rommel's famed Panzer core for the first time sums this attitude, "Rommel, you magnificent bastard, I read your book!" Before the invasion of Normandy, Patton read books on war tactics written by his opponents, Guderian and Rommel. Using their own tactics against them, Patton defeated the Germans, even though they had better tanks, more weapons and more soldiers. (See Supplement)

On the other hand, General George Armstrong Custer's battle of Little Bighorn is known as "Custer's Last Stand." The general was offered guns, but declined, saying they would slow down his regiment. Custer also declined the offer of additional cavalry, insisting that his regiment could handle whatever they encountered. He scoffed at warnings from scouts who said that one of the largest Native American encampments was waiting along the river. In the end, when the soldiers encountered the encampment, it took 2000 warriors just three hours to completely annihilate Custer and his battalion of 211 men. The general neglected his "homework," and he did not learn from the knowledge of others. His ego was so large that he believed his own "hype" – that he was invincible and did not need the advice or help of others. A valuable lesson from this event is that ego and ignorance are closely linked.

Strategies and their underlying tactics are focused on helping a company attain its specific goals and overall mission. Strategies define the overall approach that will be employed; tactics define the specific actions that will be taken to support such strategies.

To begin, it is critically important to define your "Brand Strategy," because your brand is arguably your most valuable piece of intellectual property. Every business and person has a "brand." Some were proactive in deciding what they wanted this image to be and guided it accordingly; some just let matters prevail. There are many good books on branding and you can search them at your convenience. Your brand is critical to your success. You need to establish and manage it accordingly.

Your brand is the mind impression a person gets when they see or hear your name, see your product, or notice your logo. Brands are experienced based. The image a person perceives for your product and business is comprised of the total encounters they have had relating to you, your company and your product. This includes past experience with purchasing, your advertising and promotional efforts, press articles, news stories, customer service, and word-of-mouth from other people's experiences.

Everything your business does, and everything others do or say about your business or products affects your brand. Building a brand that will allow your business to achieve its goals takes careful planning and execution; the brand and your mission must be in sync. For example: Sony® (early 1950's) *"Our mission is to become the company most known for changing the worldwide poor-quality image of Japanese products."* Sony's brand positioned all exported products as very high quality, and supported each offering with excellent service. As Sony succeeded in establishing its brand, the company was also successful at attaining its mission. A company's brand is read both externally by customers and internally by employees. Businesses that link branding strategies to the company mission take advantage of a common focus and the synergy it creates.

If your business is not careful about the creation of your brand, the media will do it for you. In The Fall of Advertising and the Rise of PR, Al and Laura Reis[14] articulate the impact the media can and will have on your brand and your overall business performance. They offer stories that show how the media made or broke businesses by impacting a brand image. One of the most blatant examples of media impact is what CBS's 60 Minutes® did to the German auto manufacturer, Audi®, in the U.S. market.

In 1986, "60 Minutes" aired a report on the Audi 5000 claiming that several people were killed when the Audi accelerated on its own when parked. The program was unable to duplicate the problem, and actually hired a consultant who modified the transmission to try to replicate the issue. As you can imagine, this caused Audi sales to plummet in the United States. The National Highway Traffic Safety Administration later ruled that the accidents were actually caused by owners pressing the accelerator instead of the brake pedal. CBS later issued a partial retraction, but the damage had already been done.[15]

Your brand is the driving force of all of the strategies you will create. Every strategic move you now make will impact it accordingly. There are six key strategies that every business must address.

Strategies:
- Product Strategy
- Pricing Strategy
- Advertising Strategy
- Promotion Strategy
- Distribution Strategy
- Support Strategy

For every individual strategy discussion to follow, there are multiple books written that provide an expansive amount of information, so this discussion will address a base-level knowledge for what you should consider. I urge you to investigate all strategies and to learn them thoroughly so that you truly understand how they work together to improve performance.

Creating business strategies that work together is like creating music on a six-string guitar. Someone can teach you to play a simple song without you really knowing how to "play."

THE RIGHT INGREDIENTS

To really learn how to cause the guitar to produce music requires much more dedication and practice.

Product Strategies – Your product strategy or strategies were identified in your "Strategic Fit" analysis. At that point, you determined exactly what product (with what benefits) was necessary to be successful. In doing so, you also determined your brand position. Now you must offer products that are absolutely consistent with a chosen position.

You may have decided that you are (will be) positioned as the company that provides the most benefit and also carries the highest price. Your strategy statement might be as follows. "*Our product strategy will be to provide products that exceed the functional, long-term performance, and aesthetic benefits of all competitors, positioning our company as the high-value leader in this product category.*"

Your specific tactics would include:
- Product design, performance, packaging, and warranty benefits for each product or product category.
- Product family management – what products are leaving, including why and when; what new products will emerge (why and when).

Offering a consistent level of products is critical to building a strong brand. Offering products that do not fit your brand can have negative consequences. If you are a premium product provider, deciding to offer a more middle-market product can impact your brand.

In 1984, Mercedes® introduced the 190E to the U.S. market, its first entry into a mid-priced luxury vehicle. Until that time,

Mercedes held a single-brand position in the U.S. as an elite, premium-quality auto manufacturer. If you asked someone what they drove and they said a Mercedes, you had an immediate impression of that person's success and status. Such reaction continues to be the core of the Mercedes Brand, but with the introduction of the 190E, something else happened.

Now, when you asked what someone drove and they said "a Mercedes," you had to ask them a second question, "Which model?" Mercedes made a decision to capture a new consumer demographic and blurred its U.S. brand image in the process. Cadillac® did something very similar with the Cimarron. Mercedes was ultimately successful with the 190E and the models it later became, but significant marketing efforts and continual product improvements were required. Cadillac was less successful, with the Cimarron holding the position as one of TIME Magazine's 50 Worst Cars of All Time[16]. It was dropped in 1988, just six years after introduction.

If your brand is an economical mid-market provider, then deciding to offer a premium-quality product under the brand will also be problematic. In 2002, Volkswagen® introduced the Phaeton, a premium quality, luxury vehicle in the $60,000 - $100,000 U.S. price range, aimed directly at Mercedes, Audi, BMW®, and Lexus®. The vehicle was well engineered, sported great styling, but had one major problem - a VW® logo on the grill. In the U.S., if you were going to spend that kind of money on a vehicle, would it be one with a VW logo on the grill? The reason most buyers would not do so would be a testament to the powerful brand created by Volkswagen over the previous decades.

Founded in 1938 by Adolf Hitler and Ferdinand Porsche, Volkswagen ("Peoples wagon") was created around building a high-quality economical vehicle for the masses. Its traditional

VW "bug," introduced in post WWII Germany, was an industry phenomenon and a worldwide success. With this dominance came the creation of the brand that ultimately would limit Volkswagen's ability to successfully compete in the premium category.

The Phaeton was subsequently dropped from the US market in 2006, after a total of 2,253 units were sold in 2004 and 2005 combined. Volkswagen has announced that it will reintroduce the Phaeton to the US market in 2009, but based on its brand image, and the shape of the U.S. economy in 2009, I will predict limited success.[17]

If you want to cross brand categories, it can be done effectively. Toyota® did it successfully with Lexus. Founded in 1989, Lexus is now the number one manufacturer of premium luxury vehicles in the U.S. Honda® also made the shift with its Acura® Brand, as did Nissan® with Infinity®. It takes the establishment of new brands, and products that match that brand, to make such cross-overs work most effectively.

Note here that the best technology does not always win. In the video recording arena, most technologists will tell you that Beta format has always been superior to VHS in recording quality; yet it was VHS that first provided the ability to record longer programs. And it was that capability, not the quality of the recording, which the consumer market wanted.

Effectively marketing the right product at the right time wins!

In the case of the VCR, effectively marketing the ability to record for two hours, and then six hours, captured a consumer market that was interested primarily in recording time, not quality.

Your product strategy needs to define the right product and to satisfy the right user at the right time. When it comes to technology, remember that the devices with the greatest benefit may have the least difficult user interface, making the technology transparent.

Pricing Strategies – Your pricing strategy was determined in your "Strategic Fit" analysis. At that point, you determined exactly what price for what level of benefits was necessary to be successful. You also determined your brand position. Now you must price your products consistent with the chosen positioning.

You may have decided, once again, that you are positioned as the high-value provider (most benefit and the highest price), so your strategy statement might be: "*Our pricing strategy is to provide pricing on all products that exceeds competition by twenty percent, positioning our company as the high-value leader in this product category.*" This strategy will clearly send a message to the market that you consider yourself to be the best.

Pricing in many businesses is a financial exercise. You have "this much overhead" so you need "this much revenue" at "this margin" to make a profit. The pricing gets adjusted accordingly. I served as the sales executive in a company where in order to get an increase in the year-to-year sales revenue for the parent company we simply put in a price increase. We then spent the following year fighting to get the same unit volume; the process ultimately failed.

Pricing is a very strategic component of your brand and plan. Your price tells the buyer how you feel about your product, as it relates to available options. Think you have the best product? If your price doesn't bear it out, you will have a difficult time getting buyers to believe it. Consumers have been taught, "You get what you pay for." Building a business plan by providing the best product at the lowest price is only going to work if you are introducing technology that changes the overall cost to deliver greater benefits. Your price needs to be established strategically, based upon your "Strategic Fit" and brand position. If you need to provide an incentive for early adoption, then provide it in the form of a one-time discount, or better yet, an extended warranty or a free service plan that does not impact the selling price and value position.

Remember this about pricing. Buyers make purchase decisions when the perceived benefit they are receiving equals or exceeds the price they are paying. When this transpires, the buyer feels like they received adequate benefit for their money (good value). When they do not think they received enough benefit (bad value), they get buyer's remorse, for which we all can relate. Your job is to provide the benefits needed to justify your price so the buyer wins. At the same time, you will need to make sure the price *also* generates a profit for your business.

There is no such thing as a standard pricing model. You will hear people talk about traditional Keystone models in the retail world where the selling price is two times the wholesale price. There are cost-plus models, target return models, and many others that focus primarily on financial performance. I am, however, a firm believer in value pricing, where it is the customer and market positioning that dictates the selling price. In today's competitive world, buyers discriminate more, demand more, and have more to choose from. Your price needs to speak to them, and lower is not always better.

A seminar attendee came up to me after an event and told me this story. There is a hand-made horse riding boot manufacturer in Iowa. One year, the owner decided to attend a premier horse show in Arizona and to display his boots for sale. In the first two days he sold basically nothing. On the last day, he roughly doubled his prices on everything, thinking he could recover some expense if he sold only a few. He sold everything that day. Why? The clientele at this particular show was very wealthy and only interested in high-quality specialty products. In his first attempt, the consumers simply rejected the product's assumed quality, based upon the price. When the price was raised to a point that peaked their interest, he was able to show the hand-made detail. Both the seller and the buyer walked away feeling like they had made a good transaction.

There are many stories about how raising price helped improve sales, and there are many about how lowering the price was prudent. The key message is that pricing is a strategic component of your success, and you need to treat it in a strategic manner.

Your specific strategy should identify:
- Target end-user selling price based on "Strategic Fit" analysis
- Target distribution margins
- Target cost to produce (COGS) – based on the required benefits and volume projections
- Target gross margins (net sales minus COGS)

- Identified price promotions (tactics) that you intend to use to promote the sale of the product

Distribution Strategies – Your distribution strategy can also be extracted from your "Strategic Fit" analysis. How your product moves from manufacturer to the end user is a strategic decision. There a many choices: direct sales representatives, independent sales representatives, in-house or contracted telesales, direct web sales, e-tailers, direct marketing, distributors, dealers, and other options.

Distribution is not a cost-based strategy, and third-party distribution is not necessarily cheaper. Like your product and pricing strategies, your distribution strategy must support your brand and mission. The environment where a product is available for sale, the amount of professional sales expertise provided for the sale, the type of products surrounding and being compared to your product, all these factors speak to your brand and its ability to sell.

When determining what channels make the most sense, note that the greater the amount of "selling" required to make a sale, the more likely it is that you will need to own the sales organization. Traditional one-step (dealer or rep) and two-step (distributor / dealer) channels make a living offering multiple manufacturers' products for sale. They put products in their catalogs or on their shelves; put up signage and window displays on occasion, many times charging a slotting fee in the process. The manufacturer, however, is still responsible for establishing the brand and generating demand.

Traditional two-step distribution costs the manufacturer between 55% and 65% of the retail price in discounts, commissions, and fees, and that does not include the advertising and promotional expense to create demand. If you are creating a retail product that you want distributed through traditional "two-step" channels, figure between five and seven times its manufactured cost at a minimum for a suggested retail price when you are doing your analysis.

In general, direct sales teams (personnel that work directly for you) are more effective as the amount of required "selling" increases. More selling work is required:

- As the sales price rises and the decision becomes more considered.
- As the sales cycle lengthens and number of contacts increases.
- As the technical complexity of the product increases and the amount of knowledge transfer needed expands.
- When the product is a new category entrant and the prospect has no experience with the product or its value.
- When the company brand is a new market entrant and the prospect has no experience with the business and its capability.

In general, third-party channels (retailers, e-tailers, dealers, manufacturers representatives) work better when the amount of required "selling" is reduced. Less selling work is required:

- As the price gets lower and the decision becomes less considered.
- As the sales cycle becomes more immediate.
- As the complexity of the product is reduced and value is more clear.
- As the need or demand for the product increases.
- As the brand becomes more established.

These are general rules, and what will work best for you must be based upon on your "Strategic Fit" analysis. One must clearly understand the level of coverage and expertise required to cause customer purchase transactions. It may be that you will use multiple channels at one time; it may be that you will start with one type and gradually expand to others. You may use one form in one market or country and a different method in another. Distribution is a very strategic decision; all forms require investment, and the worst thing you can do is to make that investment in the wrong channel(s).

If we continue with our high-value example, and presuming that your product is a business-to-business product that requires significant capital investment and has a long sales cycle, your strategy statement might be as follows: "*Our distribution strategy will be to make our products available to our target clients in North America through direct field sales representatives supported by an inside prospect qualification and sales administration team. Outside of North America, our products will be represented by a certified dealer channel, and this network will be managed and supported by an international sales executive and sales administration support team. Specific organizational structure and incentive compensation tactics are outlined as follows.*"

Advertising Strategies – Your advertising strategy will also be directed by your "Strategic Fit" analysis, mission and brand position. Advertising's role is to support the selling process by creating a specific brand-based awareness of your product in your prospect's mind ("mind-share") or causing a prospect to take some form of action. Done correctly, prospects will seek out additional information, sales representatives will make easier cold calls, and consumers will consider the product at the point of purchase or make an immediate telephone or web purchase. In many cases, advertising simply makes a current customer feel good about a past purchase.

You have three critical decisions to make regarding advertising. The first concerns what message(s) need to be conveyed to cause the desired response. The second involves the vehicles that will be most effective in carrying that message. And third, consider how many times must the message be experienced to cause the desired response.

In regards to messages, there are three general types of desired response. First, you want the recipients to garner a specific feeling about your company or product so that when making a buying decision, and they are presented with a choice, there will be a reason or internal bias towards selecting your product. Here, you are building *mind-share or brand recognition.*

Secondly, you want the recipient to take some type of immediate purchase action, which might be to visit a retail or online outlet and then purchase your product. The result may also be to call a number and make a purchase. Lastly, you may want the viewer to seek further information and then direct them to your website, toll-free number, or other location. If you are directing prospects to your website, you might want to construct the website to self-qualify your prospects a bit, and, if still interested, submit a request for contact. This will help you make better use of your selling resources.

The messages needed to effectively cause one of these three actions can be very different. For the first, the goal is to impart a level of good feeling toward your product and your company. Testimonials, award announcements, public service investments, or other information that reinforces your brand image and position in the market.

For action two, the immediate purchase, you will need to impart a more urgent message that causes the viewer to take action. Such options include limited-time sale (e.g., while supply lasts), limited edition, latest release, and other like promotions.

For action three, causing the viewer to inquire for additional information, you will need to provide a reason for investigating. This action is mostly likely to occur if they have an immediate need that is prompted by news about a new product release, service update, testimonial, or other value-based information.

In all cases, message content is strategic and specific. While some messages can serve dual purposes, it is highly recommended that each advertisement focuses on one purpose. You see advertisements regularly where someone just compiled a list of product features in the hopes that something would catch a viewer's eye. Successful businesses spend significant time and money testing to arriving at specific messages that increase effectiveness; experts assist with the task, and you should invest similar concern.

What is most frustrating to the advertising professional is that everyone thinks they are an expert. Everyone has an opinion. Perhaps you should add some sex appeal or talk about the new features. Promote our low price; I like the color blue best. Advertising requires the same level of training and skill as any other discipline. Not everyone is an expert.

The key to choosing the advertising vehicles needed to deliver your message is to select the ones that will most effectively reach your target audience with the least amount of wasted impressions. In this way you will get the most impact per dollar spent. Businesses with limited resources cannot afford to spend money advertising to those who are not prospects, and yet they do it everyday. For every website, every publication, every catalog, every television or radio station, there is a specific viewer, listener, or reader profile. Each of those vehicles also has a media kit with the applicable data. Your job is to understand your prospective customer and match your advertising to the vehicle that fits.

When designing your website, I cannot over emphasize its importance. Nearly every advertisement, piece of literature, brochure, stationery, and business card that you produce should have your website printed on it. Nearly all advertising done today drives prospects to websites for product information, location, hours of operation, and purchases.

At a minimum:

- Your website should represent the brand image you have identified in your "Strategic Fit" analysis.
- If you want your website to generate prospects, the site must be optimized for search engines.
- Website navigation is critical. Make your site user friendly, and people will use it. Make it too fancy or difficult; they will move on. Flash front-ends slow the path to information and provide limited value to the viewer; their merit is questionable.
- Like real stores, websites should make the viewer comfortable, should create an image of the company and product, and should facilitate business.
- Your website enables you to "look" as large and as strong as any other business, regardless of your size. Do not miss the opportunity to play on a level field, created by the Internet.

In today's business world, your website has become your company's front door. In many cases your home page creates the first impression a prospective purchaser receives of your business or product. Your website is crucial to creating your image, moving a prospect closer to a purchase decision, or causing a purchase to take place. Yet many businesses treat their website with little regard. Some create it themselves or hire college interns or friends. Some businesses invest greatly to have them designed professionally and then ignore them. Websites are critical; they are living environments that require daily care, and if managed carefully and professionally, a site will provide a significant component of your business success.

You identified a specific target audience in your "Strategic Fit" analysis. Now, you can do the media research and planning yourself, you can hire a skilled employee, or retain outside talent to help you create the right message and to get your message efficiently and effectively to your target audience.

I have been amazed over the years, by the number of non-advertising people who thought they could create advertising or build websites. In doing so, they wasted significant dollars saying the wrong thing, using the wrong vehicles, and then said, "It didn't work." Like all other disciplines, advertising is a research-based science for which there are experts to help you become more successful. Get the right help and spend your money wisely.

For the high-value business-to-business example we have been using, your strategy statement might be as follows: *"Our advertising strategy will position our products as the most cost-effective long-term investment to our target prospects in support of our high-value brand position. Advertising will create a consistent flow of targeted prospects for distribu-*

tion channel follow-up. Specific media plan tactics are planned as follows."

Promotion Strategies – Promotional strategies differ from advertising in vehicle selection but the message and target must remain consistent. I define "promotional vehicles" to include all venues where prospects can either see and touch your products, or hear about them from independent sources. Typical vehicles include conventions, tradeshows, seminars, and public relations efforts. There is a specific viewer, listener, or reader profile for each event; every vehicle has media kits with that appropriate data.

Like advertising, the promotional goal is to reach the maximum number of target prospects for every dollar spent. All promotional efforts must be tied directly to your advertising strategy and brand development and then executed in unison. Get professional help to maximize your effectiveness and do not waste your money.

When considering conventions and tradeshows, most businesses fail to realize even fifty percent of the potential impact. Many purchase a booth, attend, and stand there (or worse yet sit) behind a counter or table and wait for someone to ask them a question. These people get very few leads and receive little value from the show. Others collect many leads by giving away some unrelated trinket or food item. Then they go home with those unqualified leads, only to now spend additional dollars sending out literature to people who were not interested and in making expensive qualifying calls.

If you want to maximize your show investment:
• Consider pre-show promotional efforts to drive prospects

to your exhibit.

- Be a presenter at one or more of the conference educational tracks and create an industry expert profile.
- Sponsor a meal or speaking event.
- Host a press conference.
- Host a reception for key customers or a select group of prospects.
- Provide an attraction in your booth to draw attention, like product demonstrations, a magician, a celebrity, etc.
- Train your show staff to select and qualify the best prospects so that you leave with quality leads. The total number of leads is not the goal; the total number of qualified leads is the goal. Unqualified leads increase your show expense. There are specific sales personnel who work shows well, and there are those who do not. Staff your show with the best you have and maximize your investment.
- Make a professional appearance by choosing the proper attire and do not allow your staff to eat or drink in your area.
- Hold pre-show and/or post-show meetings with the staff each day to discuss new information learned and strategy updates for the upcoming day.
- Take advantage of all show networking events to meet key contacts.

Shows and conventions are serious business. Those that treat them as such get significant value. Those that do not, which seem to be the majority, waste their money.

At a major United States defense contractor show in 2002, in the booth directly across from ours, was the perfect example of "how not to do a show." The exhibit was fine, but the booth was staffed with only one representative, who was not there much of the time. When he was present, he sat in a chair eat-

ing, feet on the table, talking on his cell phone. He ignored people unless someone had a specific question. At the end of the show, rather than packing his samples (expensive hand-held computers), he simply left the items on the table and walked away. His company was a major provider; for all their investment, the representative wasted it, and provided a very poor, lasting image to the United States military.

In regards to public relations (PR), you can increase supporting press by getting to know the editors of industry and trade publications. If you develop a solid relationship and provide quality industry data over time (and advertise with them) you will garner a greater amount of press coverage.

Remember also that the media can be as much of a problem as it is a benefit. Be very careful when asked for products for "industry tests or comparisons." Your excitement that a particular publication is interested in testing your product can be turned upside down if it is tested it in a way you did not anticipate and then reviewed poorly in their publication. Not all press is good press; make good decisions. Send out regular press updates for new product releases and awards. The media can be of great benefit to you if managed correctly, and press can also cause significant problems.

Many businesses have done an exceptional job of using promotional tactics along with a quality web page design as their only form of marketing communications. There are an incredible number of options and you need qualified help to make quality decisions. It is critical to execute an effective and coordinated advertising and promotional (marketing communications) campaign. All too often, these activities are left in the hands of those without the proper experience. Marketing communications is as important as the product itself, requiring the same level of expertise to develop and produce an effective program.

For the high-value business-to-business model we have been using, the positioning should be consistent with advertising. Your strategy statement might read as follows: "*Our promotion strategy will position our products as the most cost-effective long-term investment to our target prospects in support of our high-value brand position. The strategy will provide "hands-on" client demonstration opportunities, media testimonials and announcements, and create a consistent flow of qualified prospects for the distribution channel. Specific promotional tactics are outlined as follows.*"

Support Strategies – The ability to produce an excellent product, to price it to sell, then promote and sell it effectively can all be diminished if your business cannot provide effective, after-sale support, the last impression many customers have. No matter how good your product, there will be after-sale support needs. Whether there are questions about operation or requests for repair or return, the brand image of your business can be reinforced or destroyed with this strategy, or lack thereof.

In today's global marketplace, with the ability to purchase competitive products from multiple channels, especially online, the battleground, while still price focused, has added customer service. Purchasing products "on sale" is a given in today's market; the ability to attract customers and keep them is now more about how well you take care of them than the price paid. Long ago, the best and fastest growing online e-tailers figured out that if you can make the purchase, return, and repair process painless, you can attract and retain a loyal customer base. Several on-line retailers that have used the support strategy as a major differentiator include, Sweetwater Music Instruments, Crutchfield, Tire Rack, and Johnston & Murphy.[18]

For some companies, the after-sale support of products is so exemplary that it becomes their market differentiator. Sears® built the Craftsman® tool line on one simple promise – "if it ever breaks, we will replace it, no questions asked." Toyota built the Lexus Brand with a unique service plan; for all needs, a new Lexus loaner vehicle is brought to the customer. Your car is taken in for service and delivered back to you at the place of your choosing. Surely you can name companies with which you will continue to do business and those with whom you will not, based solely upon the after-sale support you received.

Whether you are selling retail goods, services, or high-dollar capital equipment, your customers have options. Executing all of the previous strategies as needed to gain new customers can be wasted if you cannot keep them satisfied. Will you train third party resellers to service your product or will you offer only in-house service and support? Will you offer support on-site or online? Will help be available 24/7 or only during regular business hours? Will you accept returns for any reason? No matter what you choose, your support strategy must fit the brand image and market position from your "Strategic Fit" analysis.

For the high-value business model we have been using, the positioning should be the same, and your strategy statement might read as follows: *"Our support strategy will provide customer and channel support programs in line with our overall quality brand image. We will provide support on a 24 x7 basis, both online and with live customer representatives. We will also provide operational support, repair, replacement, or refund options as needed to ensure 100% customer satisfaction. Specific supporting staff, programs and tactics are offered as follows."*

In my later years at Universal® Gym Equipment, Inc., as Director of Sales and Marketing, I had the responsibility for customer service operations. Under a new parent company, we were continually forced to reduce expenses in an effort to improve profitability, regardless of the customer impact. Universal grew to be one of the top manufacturers of fitness equipment in the world by making products that worked well, were durable, and easy to support.

But the addition of aerobic equipment like bikes, treadmills, stair climbers, and rowing machines brought computer electronics to the industry. With electronics came a level of technical support that went far beyond what was once needed. No longer could you simply sell a fitness club or school a new pulley or cable. Now you had to diagnose an electrical issue with a non-skilled employee and hopefully send the right part.

Compounding this problem was the growth in popularity of treadmills; at that time they were the most difficult products to keep operating. The constant friction between the running belt and the bed of the treadmill as well as the dirt build-up eventually caused a significant load on the electronics and frequent failures. It was not uncommon to go to a large club and see a line of twenty Universal treadmills with "out-of-order" signs posted on half of them. The real problem was that early models were not designed to be easily serviced or to withstand the level of required use. So, Universal had a product that started to diminish its once strong brand. In reaction to the problem, it seemed logical to expand the customer service department with an adequate number of qualified technicians to handle the problems until a new design could be employed, but that is not what happened.

The new parent company, in its desire to improve profit-ability, continued to cut budgets (and related staffing) to the point that if you called electronic customer service, the average on-hold time to get a technician grew to over thirty minutes. If you got frustrated and hung-up, you simply had to get back in queue at a later time. Every technician knew that each call they were answering had a customer who had been waiting for over half an hour.

Needless to say, Universal's brand was significantly dam-aged by the parent company's myopic view of the profit line. New competitors with better products and support programs emerged, and today after being sold multiple times, Universal is a fraction of its former presence.

Strategy Summary – The six strategies mentioned can be dissected and studied in depth; multiple books exist for any of the six subjects, and I would encourage you to read one or more. Our discussion here emphasizes that all parts are critical. You must understand that strategies require founda-tion, balance, and expertise to maximize your ability to suc-ceed. It is not any single strategy or decision; it is a balanced "Recipe" of all elements that wins.

RECIPE CHECK: BUSINESS PLAN

Strategies and their related tactics, when established correctly and executed effectively, are the keys to attaining your goals.

- Make sure all strategies are focused on your mission, and specifically on the plan's goals and objectives.

- Make sure your strategies are realistic and that you will have the resources needed to execute them effectively.
- Make sure you give strategies time to work, but do not be complacent about ones that are clearly not working.
- Make sure you get professional help when needed.

Operations Plan

This section outlines how you will handle the operational components of your business. If you view your entire organization holistically, the operations plan, if well coordinated, will allow you to operate effectively and efficiently. If, on the other hand, you simply react to operational issues when the need arises, you will learn many painful lessons. At a minimum, you should be able to outline the following plans:

- Accounting plan:
  - Accounting system application and procedures
  - Tax plan
  - Reporting and record keeping infrastructure and policies
  - Benefits and insurance programs
  - Banking relationship / financing plan
  - Equity investment plan (if needed)
  - Long-term capital plan
  - Annual budgeting / forecasting plan
  - Internal controls plan (theft control)
- Production / manufacturing plan:
  - In-house and / or outsourced production
  - Overhead and labor structure
  - Performance guidelines: warranty, delivery, labor variance, re-work, etc.
- Materials and inventory plan:
  - Manufacturing requirements planning (MRP) application

- - Vendor relationship plan, including backup vendor plans
  - Performance guidelines: inventory turns, scrap, obsolete, returns, etc.
- Order entry / processing plan:
  - Order entry application and process
  - Performance guidelines: time to process, accuracy, etc.
- Prospect and client management:
  - Contact management application and procedure
  - Other customer relationship management (CRM) applications; customer service, technical service, etc.
  - Performance guidelines: time to contact, time to fulfill, satisfaction, etc.
- Organizational plans:
  - Staffing plan (FTEs, PTEs, contractors, interns, etc.)
  - Compensation plans
  - Employee manual
  - Job descriptions
  - Annual evaluation plan
  - Board / advisor plan

All of these plans and tools are essential to attain your mission, goals and objectives. If you hire the right talent, the experience and expertise required to create and execute these plans in detail will come.

Financial Plan

In this section, you must outline projected performance based specifically on all components of the marketing and operations plans. If you are an ongoing business, you must also compare past performance to your future projections.

Historical performance, when compared to projected performance, should clearly indicate financial effects of the plan. Do not err by showing significant improvement in projections if your plan does not clearly outline viable reasons for such change. Do not simply plan for lineal growth; likewise, do not plan for growth to come all at once if strategic activities do not support it. Such activity will not happen, and any capital resource you are courting will see the miscalculations.

Your financials must track directly to the plan you have written. Your financial plan is not your business plan; it is the result of your business plan. If done properly, it will delineate the resources needed as well as the projected outcomes.

When speaking of financials, I am continually amazed by the number of business CEOs who lack understanding, simply relying on a CFO or controller. Early in my career, as a sales and marketing executive, I was forced to read, project, and understand financials because it was the only language our parent company could speak. If I needed to be persuasive with my sales or marketing plan, the data had to be based in financials. I learned it begrudgingly, and it was one of the best learning experiences of my career.

If you are going to be a leader you must understand the financial plan and your performance against that plan. You must be able to explain numbers to your team, banker, investors, and most importantly, be comfortable with them yourself. You must be able to read and compare balance sheets, statements of income, and cash flow on a monthly basis. You must compare data to projections and past performance, and have the contrast mean something. You must understand how these statements affect your overall plan, as well as the necessary changes they will indicate.

Good financial performance does not just happen; it is a result of good planning and understanding or a lack thereof. *In the past, I served as a new board member of a local busi-*

THE RECIPE FOR BUSINESS SUCCESS

ness during the 2001 downturn. At my second meeting, I was pointing out potential year-end cash shortfalls and the need to take corrective action. The chairman told me –"you can't worry about the numbers; they're going to be what they are and to leave it alone." Well, they were what they were, the business had the large shortfall, and the bank nearly got the keys. The result was due to a group of successful businessmen who simply did not understand financials and the story they tell.

Business leaders who leave the numbers to others, or who subscribe to the checkbook accounting method, "that if there is money in the account, we must be doing fine," are the ones whose businesses do not grow or fail. You do not need to be a CPA (Certified Public Accountant) to learn how to project, read, and adjust course based on financial information.

Your financial projections and comparisons should include:
- Income statements:
  - Past three years on an annual basis. These should show enough detail in the revenue and expense categories to compare to your projected numbers.
  - Projected three years with the upcoming year on a monthly basis:
    - If you are going to generate losses for more than the upcoming year, it is recommended that you show your monthly budget for each of the three years.
    - Your projected statements must be based upon the work completed to date in your "Strategic Fit" and business plan.
      - Revenue numbers will tie back to your goals, which are tied to strategies.
      - Cost of goods sold (COGS) and the resulting gross margin, which will tie back to your product

and pricing strategies.

- Expenses will link to your strategies and operational plans.
- Note: Projected changes from historical trends must be explained by, and relate to, the plan.

- Cash-flow statements:
  - Projected three years, with the upcoming year, on a monthly basis:
    - If you are going to be "burning cash" for more than the upcoming year, it is recommended that you show your monthly budget for each of the three years.
  - If you have done a wise job of planning and projecting up to this point, then your cash-flow statement will indicate the maximum capital you will need and when you will need it:
    - It may also be helpful to include a graph with your spreadsheet indicating your cash needs by month.
    - When securing needed capital, make sure you secure at least 125% of the maximum number indicated to offset unforeseen fluctuations in your plan.

- Balance sheets:
  - Past three years (year end)
  - Projected three years

- Annual comparisons:
  - Look at enough comparisons to provide comfort with trends and projections. If your gross margin (GM) is eroding annually, or if your development expense is growing over time, you can then see it, research it, understand it, and make needed corrections.

Example comparison chart:

Year	2006 act	2007 act	2008 act	2009 pro	2010 pro	2011 pro
Revenue	$1,000	$2,000	$4,000	$6,000	$10,000	$15,000
COGS	40%	40%	45%	45%	45%	45%
GM	60%	60%	55%	55%	55%	55%
Expenses	43%	45%	47%	47%	46%	47%
Sales & Marketing	20%	20%	22%	21%	20%	20%
Development	8%	10%	10%	10%	10%	10%
Support	6%	6%	6%	6%	6%	6%
IT	2%	2%	2%	2%	2%	2%
Warranty	1%	1%	1%	1%	1%	1%
G&A	6%	6%	6%	7%	7%	8%
NOP	17%	15%	8%	8%	9%	8%

In the above example, net operating profit (NOP) is eroding based upon both increasing expenses and reduced gross margins, typical of many expanding businesses. If you are watching this trend, you can validate the specific reason and understand if there is anything you can do to improve it. Notice that the example plan calls for the erosion to stop and profits to level out, not increase. If this is what you are projecting, you must be able to substantiate why it will occur.

- Capital plan: Outline of projected capital purchases. These are tied to cash flow statements for each year of your historical and projected income statements. Typical capital investments include:
  - Facilities (buildings, furniture, etc.)
  - Equipment (machinery, vehicles, etc.)
  - Information Technology (computers, software, etc.)
  - Development (R&D which can be capitalized)
- Covenant plan: Your bank covenants, if any, are critical to

maintaining your lending instruments. Understand your covenants and plan for them.

- Budgeting plan: Quality businesses update their business plans and related budgets annually. Creating quality budgets for the upcoming year requires a disciplined process and complete team acceptance. Do not simply add on to your past budget. Take the approach commonly called "*zero-based budgeting*." Build your budgets from scratch including only what is necessary to accomplish your plan. Far too many businesses carry old programs and their related expenses forward, all of which are not needed, driving up their operating costs and wasting critical cash resources.

I recommend the following budgeting process:
- First, update the business plan, including all strategies.
- To establish your revenue goals, present your updated product, pricing, advertising, promotion, and support strategies to your sales leadership.
- Get your sales leadership and organization to create a projected sales forecast, by product and by month, which is based upon your strategies. You should be very careful that the sales organization drives the forecasting process so that they are fully engaged in attaining the number. If you impose a projection, they will not "own it," and you will not achieve it.
- Work with the sales organization to arrive at a number that works for both the business and the sales organization.
- Once you have finalized the sales forecast and marketing strategies, you can then ask your operations teams to create their projected budgets based upon attaining the forecasted revenue, products, and timing. Like the

sales organization, you want individual, operational departments to arrive at their own initial budgets, again creating buy-in and ownership.

- Once you have all the departmental budgets, you can then compile the projected income statements and view the results. Clearly some adjusting will be necessary. If the budget does not roll up to a workable model, do not simply change a single line item to make it look better. Go back to each department leader and build a revised plan. If you involve the entire team in the process, you will arrive at a budget that everyone owns, making goals much easier to attain.
- Once you have a final, projected income statement, you can generate the cash-flow statement and balance sheet.
- The budget process may take several weeks; I have traditionally started the process in October of each year with the goal to be complete by the middle of November, allowing proper time to begin timely execution for the following year.

• Funding plan: Securing third-party funding, like everything else we have discussed, is a process that requires expert preparation, skill and execution. Whether you need start-up capital or capital to fund expanding operations, if you need other people's money to grow your business, you need to be prepared. See the "Resource Chapter" for significant additional information.

Good financial planning comes from having the right information and the ability to use it. Critical to this process is selecting a qualified, outside accounting firm to augment needed skills and specialties. The firm should provide the depth of services required for your type of business; interview them, get references, and select a quality business partner.[19]

Monitoring Plan

Assuming now that you are going to use your plan to operate a business and not just set it aside, how often will you review the plan and your related performance? Who will you include in that review? How often will you make adjustments or amendments to the plan? I recommend that you, your leadership team, and your advisors review your performance as follows:

Monthly:
- Review your financial performance against plan and highlight variances with explanations accordingly:
  - Income statement plan versus actual with variance
  - Cash flow statement plan versus actual with variance
  - Balance sheet
- Review key scheduled action performance against plan. Did you do all the things in the month that were anticipated and if not, why not?

Quarterly:
- Same monthly reviews as above.
- Review your assumptions and critical issues for validity.
- Review your goals for validity.
- Review your strategies for effectiveness.
- Review your operational plans for effectiveness.
- On a quarterly basis you should be thinking about the overall validity of your plan and making adjustments or amendments. Have market impacts changed? Did you fail to get something done that was critical to success?

Did a competitor do something unexpected? Waiting too long to make changes in the face of change can be fatal to your business.

In the year 2001, when I was leading the computer-telephony company, we started with an aggressive expansion plan, coming from a huge growth in the business in 2000. The communications industry's climate had been changing since mid 2000. Our business was still strong and growing, but the market was giving more than adequate signs to be wary. We started the year by refraining from planned capital spending or new hires until the end of the first quarter. In March, I attended the Internet World Show, usually the busiest show in the industry, and found that roughly thirty percent of the exhibit space, although pre-sold, was unoccupied by last minute cancellations. When the show opened, the traffic in the aisles was all I needed to see. I remember calling back to our CFO, from the second story of our brand new exhibit booth, asking her to start working on a revised plan.

Between March and July, the leadership team created multiple new plans as the industry tanked. Staffing was cut; capital projects were scrapped. Department budgets were zero-based and updated for the new environment; overall strategies were revised. Multiple times in the revision process, the challenge was made to wait a couple months before significant adjustments were made and to see if the market rebounded. We did not wait, and at the end of that year, which also added terrorism to the impact, we ended up with a fraction of the original sales plan, but our net performance was positive. Many companies that failed to react did not fare as well, and my old business remains vital today.

Consistent monitoring of your plan and the capability to

react to change in a timely manner can save your business. This is not to say that you should make "knee-jerk" modifications and reduce your focus. Clearly, the decision to make changes in your plan needs to be validated and acted on with the best possible data and counsel.

Action Plan

To facilitate your monthly and quarterly monitoring, and to clearly attach responsibility to your entire team, create a month-to-month action plan. Indicate the key actions to be taken, who is responsible, and the date of required completion. Include all the key strategic and operational tactics (actions) outlined in your plan. Once complete, this action plan will allow your entire leadership team to understand how their actions combine with other department actions to create a successful outcome. The action plan also holds employees accountable to their peers.

In my experience, if you hold regular monitoring sessions with your team, "*peer pressure*" will be a stronger incentive than "*boss pressure*" for attainment of completed actions. No team member wants a report in front of his or her peers that indicates they personally did not complete actions, especially if such impacted company performance. If your leadership incentive plan is tied to overall company performance, this process will prove exceptionally effective.

JANUARY		
ACTION	RESPONSIBLE	DATE REQUIRED
Advertisement in X magazine	Jim	1/5
Product X released to production	John	1/15
Sales rep for eastern region hired	Sue	1/31
New MRP system operational	Bill	1/31

RECIPE CHECK: BUSINESS PLAN

A quality business plan provides the strategic and tactical foundation for consistent success and keeps leadership focused on business priorities. The plan is a living document; if reviewed and amended on a regular basis, it provides guidance needed for ongoing success.

- The executive summary tells the "cover jacket" story of your business. It is concise, compelling and honest.
- The mission and principles identify your brand, end game, and culture you will employ to reach both annual and long-term goals.
- The "Strategic Fit" analysis is the foundation of your business plan. It validates your business model and identifies why you can be successful.
- Your assumptions and critical issues will make you think about the overall business environment and help build a more robust, defendable business.
- Your goals and objectives will be based upon your "Fit" and mission and at all times be specific, measurable, attainable, relevant and timely.
- Your strategies will have strong foundations and be consistent in focusing on attainment of financial, brand and mission goals.
- Your operational plans will provide an effective and efficient business engine that will attain financial, brand and mission goals.
- Your financials section will identify resources necessary to attain financial, brand and mission goals as well as the resulting outcomes.
- Your monitoring plan will ensure that key leadership will operate the business with the best and most timely information. It will also allow for strategic and operational enhancements and amendments as needed to attain financial, brand and mission goals.

- Your action plan will identify key strategic and operational actions needed to attain financial, brand and mission goals, as well as the responsible stakeholders.

SCORE YOUR BUSINESS

At this point – take a moment and score your business on page 185. If you can truly say that you have a business plan as outlined, score yourself at ten. If you can identify some of the components but still need to work on others, score yourself accordingly. If you simply cannot identify any component of your plan, score yourself a zero. Your scoring will allow you to identify opportunities for improved performance, so grade yourself honestly.

THE RIGHT EXECUTION

TALENT
The Right People in the Right Places

Many, if not most businesses are talent heavy in some areas and light in others. If the business was founded by an engineer, it is common for the company to have strong engineering talent but weaknesses in other areas. Talent tends to center around the discipline and "comfort zone" of the ownership. This same talent is unaware of the capabilities it is missing, and a serious imbalance is created. Employees are hired incorrectly and people are branded with titles and responsibilities out of their expertise.

In my role with a trucking communications business, I inherited a marketing manager as one of my team. We were producing a wireless communication product in direct competition with Qualcomm® and needed a strong commercial marketing and sales team. While interviewing this person, I found out that he had been with the company for nearly twenty years. When I asked about his background, he said he had been an engineer for his entire career. I then asked when he got involved in marketing. His response was that he just recently became involved after seeing an open requisition for the marketing position he now held.

This situation was quickly remedied, but the employee saw no issue with taking a job in which he had no experience. After all, he was an engineer, how hard could marketing be? More importantly, management made the decision to offer him the job based upon the same thought process.

People would easily laugh at the thought of an NFL center switching to tight end with no experience or capabilities. The team would suffer as well. Patients would be horrified if a surgeon about to perform an open-heart procedure on them was actually a dermatologist who thought he would try cardiology. The reality is that in the business world, these types of humorous and horrifying talent mistakes are made every day. Businesses suffer greatly from incredible mismatches; no one identifies or deals with the problem.

Quality execution comes from having the right talent in the right places at the right times. The sports world understands this concept as do those who excel in the business world. Those who do not grasp the idea fail to reach their potential or simply fail altogether. Quality business talent comes from a combination of the necessary disciplines, capabilities, experience, and proper balance. Whether you need hundreds of people or only a few, building the right talent will make the journey to success smoother and faster.

Disciplines

There are six top disciplines needed to create the right "Recipe" and to perform under optimal leadership. They include:

- Marketing
- Development
- Sales
- Operations
- Information Technology (IT)
- Finance

Note: There are certainly other specialized disciplines needed within specific businesses, but these six are essential in all businesses.

Marketing

Marketing is, perhaps, the most misunderstood of all the disciplines. When you walk into most companies and ask to speak to the person in charge of marketing, you will likely be sent to either the sales or advertising department. Although sales is critically important to business success, and advertising is a subset of marketing, neither one is actually "marketing."

Marketing is the process of planning and executing the creation, pricing, promotion, and distribution of ideas, goods, and services that mutually satisfy customer and organizational objectives (American Marketing Association).[20]

Marketing is responsible for:
- Identifying and validating a "Strategic Fit" and aiming the business properly in that direction.
- Defining and managing the company's brand.
- Creating and driving the execution of the marketing plan:
  - Product Strategies. Marketing is responsible for providing the right guidance to product development. Marketing must combine strategic market needs with company capabilities to define and manage the product(s) needed to satisfy the "Fit" identified and to maximize success.
  - Pricing Strategies. Marketing is responsible for providing guidance needed to set the strategic pricing to satisfy the "Fit" and to maximize profitability.
  - Advertising and Promotion Strategies. Marketing is responsible for creating the sales opportunity through in-

creased brand awareness and prospect generation.
- Distribution Strategies. Marketing is responsible for identifying channel(s) of distribution needed to satisfy the "Fit" and to maximize revenue generation.
- Support Strategies. Marketing is responsible for identifying support levels required to satisfy the brand promise and to maximize repeat purchases.

Development

Development's responsibility is to create the products and services necessary for the business to effectively satisfy its "Strategic Fit." In a market driven business, development looks to marketing for direction on what products or services to create.

In a product driven business, products get created with little to no input from marketing. Here, marketing is truly a sales or advertising function, and management looks to marketing to sell the "genius" they have created. Products get identified by company egos, and many times, product offerings line up poorly with market needs, creating "products in search of a market." When sales revenue does not meet expectations, marketing (sales) is held responsible. After all, the product was great; it must have been marketing's inability to sell that caused poor results.

There are many examples of failed product launches and missed sales plans that are the direct result of a development team operating in a self-absorbed vacuum. Instead of working with marketing to create products for which there is a definable "Fit," development sidestepped the process in favor of their own knowledge. In the end, the company ended up with a product few wanted to buy.

The trucking communications business, who I worked for in the past, created a competitive mobile-communications offering for the long-haul trucking industry. In 1988, Qualcomm® Corp (San Diego, CA USA) introduced the first satellite-based mobile communications and vehicle tracking system (omni-TRACS®) for the transportation industry. The system, when installed in both long-haul trucks and fleet dispatch systems, allowed dispatchers to communicate directly with drivers and to locate vehicles, while in motion, in a highly cost effective manner. The technology provided nearly 100% coverage in the continental United States and allowed the dispatch center to track the location of a truck down to the nearest 100 feet.

This technological advancement, though not readily accepted by drivers or fleet owners, significantly improved business profitability, customer satisfaction, and driver satisfaction and retention. Qualcomm quickly became the market leader, penetrating the largest carriers early in the process. Other competitors, using cellular phone technology cropped up, but due to cost and coverage, were never a serious threat.

The contractor had a strong heritage in the transportation industry and decided it was going to introduce a mobile communications system that would technologically outperform Qualcomm. The product would not only catch up to them in market share, but would actually pass them, and attain a market dominant position in a relatively short period of time.

Top quality engineers developed a radio that used geostationary satellites, terrestrial based towers, and the military's GPS satellite network to provide a radio that would deliver 100% nationwide coverage. They would do this more cost effectively than Qualcomm while providing more accurate truck location information. The first production radio was introduced about the time I was hired to direct sales and marketing of the product.

I inherited the goal to surpass Qualcomm in market share, and after researching the market, I learned the following:

- *Over fifty percent of the available long-haul trucking market had already adopted Qualcomm, including nearly all of the largest fleets.*
- *Those who had adopted Qualcomm had little to no perceived issues with coverage, cost, or location capabilities.*
- *Trucking company executives were, in most cases, previous long-haul drivers that had great knowledge of trucks and trailers but did not understand (nor want to understand) radio communications.*

Before making any significant progress, it was clear that the goal was unattainable and that we had no real "Fit" in the market as we were positioned. The company truly believed that their superior radio would supplant Qualcomm's technology and that the genius of the product would win buyers. When explaining the situation in a team meeting, I was once told to get "smarter customers" and that would help.

Not long after introduction, it was discovered that the radios had a minor application defect. To locate and swap out radios on trucks spread out across the nation was not only a major task, but it cost the associated trucking fleet roughly $800 per truck to stop, retrieve, and take the vehicles off-line for a day. Less than a year after the radios were updated, a problem with the antenna was discovered; the trucks had to be taken off-line again.

Because the market was limited in size, because Qualcomm had a quality product with a nearly five year head start, and because the cost of entry was so high, the company could not establish a defendable "Fit" in the market. It never had a chance to surpass Qualcomm with its plan, and because of quality missteps, the company never had the ability to secure enough market share to attain profitability. The belief that superior technology would win customers, as well as driving technology to market ahead of proper testing, caused this venture to fail.

In a market-driven business, development must assist marketing in creating a marketing requirement document (MRD) for each and every new offering. Development must also design the final offering in cooperation with operations to minimize material and labor costs. Training of operations and sales, as well as input to marketing for new offerings or enhancements, is also expected.

Sales
Sales is the second most misunderstood or undervalued discipline of any business. Sales are expected to occur based upon the "genius" of the product. Many businesses expect sales to occur simply because they always have. The sales division in many companies is often the brunt of conversation:

- "Salespeople are just overpaid partiers."
- "If you can't get a degree in it, how important can it be?"
- "If you can't get a professional job, you can always try sales."
- "Anyone can sell. After all, how hard can it be?"

Sales is a professional discipline with equal importance to all others. Professional salespeople study as hard and as long as any other professional. There are no continuing education credits, no annual conventions, so professional salespeople must learn on their own. Sales, however, remains the top income generating profession in the world.

I was a sales trainer for a time in my career, traveling

across the globe, teaching sales representatives the difference between selling and telling. My mentor was Tom Hopkins.[21] I studied his book (<u>How to Master the Art of Selling</u>), listened to his tapes, watched his videos, and attended his live, training sessions. If you truly want to understand what it takes to be a sales professional, I encourage you to view his materials.

There are other books and professionals I learned from: <u>Strategic Selling</u> by Robert Miller and Stephen Heiman; <u>Major Account Sales Strategy</u> and <u>SPIN Selling</u> both by Neil Rackham; and the exceptional sales training capabilities of Mr. Joe Golding with Differentiation Strategies Inc.[22] All of them added to my professional capabilities, business success and income. The value a professional sales team can bring to your organization is immense; the damage and lack of value a wrong team can create is also tremendous.

CEOs and founders who start a company, inherit a company, or are trying to save a company often decide to do the sales work themselves, even though they have no professional training or resulting skills. They are the product experts. The number of companies that provide excellent products and fail to reach their potential because they do not, or will not, invest in sales professionals is staggering. I have watched many businesses fail to grow because leadership undervalued or did not understand the sales discipline. When founders keep doing sales themselves, they limit growth to what they can generate; sales people with skills and experiences that are not suitable are retained, and the company fails to grow.

Sales, like all other disciplines, requires training, expertise, and experience matched to the need of the business. If you need top quality sales professionals to convert prospects to customers, then it is critical that you hire accordingly. From my experience, I would estimate for personnel who have any kind of sales title, less than ten percent are truly sales professionals.

A typical, ineffective salesperson adopts the "sit down and shut up, while I dazzle you with how smart I am about my product and why it is good for you" selling technique. Basically "telling" instead of "selling," in the hopes that something will influence you to buy. They fail to qualify and identify if a person is a viable prospect. They fail to learn anything about a prospect's needs or wants, and fail to close the order or to move onto a better opportunity. Poor salespeople will spend years on a deal that was never going to close, when they could have moved past that suspect after the first or second contact.

The next time you encounter someone whom you believe is a sales professional, ask him or her, "What is the most important part of the selling process?" The answer must be related to understanding prospects' needs as they relate to their product. I once held up a $100 bill at sales training programs and would offer it to the first person who could tell me the most important benefit of their product. You would be surprised how many different features and benefits were blurted out trying to win that money, but all failed. The winning answer is, "The one that is most important to the customer."

Sales' primary responsibility is to cause your target prospects to make a purchase decision in favor of your product or service. The required capability, value, and investment in and by your sales organization expands as the selling work required to make a sale increases.

The responsibilities of the sales organization include:
• Prospect identification and/or qualification

- Sales process management:
  - Identification of needs/problems
  - Establishing value around those needs
  - Closing the order
- Sales transaction processing:
  - Order entry process/transmission of customer requirements to operations
- CRM (Customer Relationship Management)
- Sales forecasting:
  - Initial component of business MRP (Manufacturing requirements planning)
- Customer input to marketing for product development or marketing communications

In my experience, finding, hiring, and retaining top quality sales personnel is the most difficult staffing challenge any business faces. Equally, if not more difficult, is securing the right sales leaders, the ones who can assemble and lead a top sales organization. *The key to maximizing sales revenue for your company is understanding your selling needs and environment, and then building the right team.*

Your sales team will likely be your most significant investment on a per member basis. You must value the required talent and pay what is necessary to get it. If you are not a professional sales leader, you should retain one and let him or her build your sales team.

Operations
Operations, which includes the production, procurement and delivery of your products, has the responsibility to:
- Deliver the sold product on time to the customer by managing:

- All vendor/provider relationships to ensure that all components or services are available when needed.
- Production timing and schedules to guarantee resources are available to make products or deliver services.
- Order acceptance to verify that orders are placed correctly.

• Deliver the purchased product to the customer, on margin, by managing:
- Amount of labor content.
- Vendor material costs.
- Inventory turns (to minimize obsolete material and reduce capital employed).
- Facility overhead.
- Scrap and re-work.
- Warranty expense.

• Deliver the sold product, on quality, by managing:
- Transition to production from development.
- Culture of the production team.
- Quality of production materials.
- Quality of vendor relationships.

In many businesses, operations is also responsible for after-sale customer support. This includes telephone support, on-site service, and related fulfillment. The quality of the customer experience regarding after-sale support has, perhaps, the greatest impact on the lasting impression of your brand.

Operations, like all other disciplines, have a significant impact on your brand and your overall ability to maximize success. On time, on margin and on quality must all be done together to insure satisfied customers and profitable performance. Many companies have succumbed to prioritizing the process of reducing costs and improving efficiencies at the expense of the product and customer. This type of thinking can damage the company brand and revenue performance in the process.

In 1967 AMF® purchased the ailing Harley Davidson Motorcycles®, ending 62 years of private family ownership. In an effort to fix the company's financial problems, AMF was determined to significantly increase the speed and volume of motorcycle production to compete with the new influx of Japanese motorcycles. For the first time in Harley's history, the AMF logo appeared alongside the Harley logo on each bike, creating an immediate brand problem. In its efforts to increase production speed to compete with the likes of Honda®, AMF introduced high throughput manufacturing processes, and ultimately drove the business away from its quality standards.

During the AMF era, Harleys became known as "leakers." The engines actually leaked oil onto the floor in dealer showrooms and customer garages. The poor quality and re-branding impacted revenues to the degree that the company nearly went bankrupt. In 1981, thirteen Harley Davidson managers bought the company back from AMF.[23]

Although the brand took years to rebuild, Harley now enjoys the reputation on which it was founded; the story of this incredible turn around is well chronicled in the book Well Made in America by Peter Reid.[24]

Information Technology (IT)

IT is responsible for providing data and communications services that allow a business to operate effectively and efficiently both internally and for your customers. Although a relatively new discipline to the optimal business "Recipe," IT has become central to the effectiveness of all the other disciplines.

Information technology was initially thought of as a utility, managed by other departments. "The server's down" was akin to the "the power is out" or "the water is off." You called the appropriate service organization and had the problem resolved. In the case of IT, because of the number and nature of "issues," most companies added a specialist to the team, a person who usually reported to the finance department.

As IT became more integral to company performance, customer satisfaction, and overall brand image, information technology became a critical discipline of its own. Companies that fail to evolve technologically will fall further behind the competition.

Internally, IT is responsible for:
- Workstation and server / network operation.
- Application development, procurement, training, and management.
- Disaster recovery and data backup.
- Telecommunications, including all phone-related products and technologies.

Externally, IT is responsible for:
- Web access.
- Electronic customer interaction – Electronic Data Interchange (EDI), service, etc.
- Incoming call management.

The expectation of employees and customers to seamlessly access data needed to make decisions (in real time) has become standard. The ability to make such activity happen in a way that requires the least amount of "technology" effort by the user is the competitive battleground.

The Internet is now a component of every business and is

the complete venue for many web-based enterprises. A company's web page has now become its front door; purchases, customer service, technical support, brand management, and product procurement are all transacted and impacted online. Your overall IT strategy is critical, and with the pace of evolving technology and its impact on your overall business performance, information technology can no longer be managed as a utility.

Finance
Finance is responsible for providing monetary guidance, general accounting and risk management.

"Financial guidance" can be described as assisting a business in making solid financially strategic decisions by providing necessary data and advice on a timely basis. It does not mean that finance should make final decisions, but rather guide the process.

The areas where finance should offer guidance include:
- Capital planning
- Capital raising
- Budgeting – departmental and total company
- Cash flow management
- Pricing/margin strategy
- Vendor relationships
- Banking and equity partner relationships
- Shareholder relationships
- Company investments
- Risk management

General accounting includes the management, reporting and interpretation of all company financial information. Traditionally, accounting is responsible for providing projected and actual income statements, balance sheets, cash-flow statements and planning. Proper accounting and timely reporting maximizes the use of funds and allows the leadership team to make corrections or course-changing decisions when necessary on a real-time basis.

In smaller companies, ones without a dedicated human resources or legal department, finance is likely responsible for managing employee benefits and the company's tax, legal, and insurance requirements. Finance must work in balance with all other disciplines and resist the urge to "drive." There are many companies who, in an effort to improve profit performance, crushed the company brand or the entire business by making financially, myopic decisions.

During the last few years of my tenure at Universal Gym Equipment, Inc., we were acquired by a British holding company known for buying businesses, cutting costs to improve earnings, and then selling off entities before the cost cutting could impact performance. The holding company was not known as a strong business operator.

At one point our parent executives called me into a meeting where they were going through my marketing budget line by line to see what they could cut. They found a line-item for our annual sales meeting and asked how the funds would be used. I told them that they were used to train our salespeople on new products, overall selling skills, etc. Their response was, "Why don't you just hire sales people who already know how to sell?"

On another occasion, the executives asked if it would be cheaper to run our advertisements in black and white rather than in color. Sarcastically, I told them, "Sure. And it would be even cheaper if we didn't run them at all." They got very excited and asked, "Could we do that" and were serious. Similar, odd questions continued over time as we struggled to do what the new owners wanted and to maintain our market position. (Note: If these questions don't sound ignorant to you, you need additional sales and marketing discipline on your team now!)

The parent executives were accountants and lawyers; their solution for everything was, "squeeze the cost." One day I said, "You keep cutting the sales and marketing budget, but keep asking for greater sales. When I finally tell you it can't be done, what's going to happen?" They said, "We'll just replace you with someone who says it can be done."

This practice leads to only one place - the death or significant retardation of a business, which is what happened to Universal. The parent company acquired it and stifled it, all the while saying it was some other problem. Businesses are not successful because of accounting, but because the right product is provided to a willing purchaser at a price that causes the sale to occur and profit to be generated. You must have good accounting, but accounting should not dictate your business. Neither should human resources (HR),legal, operations, IT or development. Your plan should drive your business.

RECIPE CHECK: BALANCED TEAM

Quality execution comes from having the right disciplines involved in your business. All these disciplines are of equal importance. When you place unequal value or importance on specific disciplines at the expense of others, you disrupt the balance of your organization, and results will suffer.

It is not necessary for you to have separate individuals for each discipline, nor is it necessary for every discipline to have a full-time employee. In many cases, a single person may possess multiple capabilities, although it is unlikely you will ever find a person that truly meets all needs. You may also balance your demands with paid consultants, advisors, or board members. Regardless of how the combination is compiled, it is essential to maximizing your business success.

To build a well-rounded team, you must provide the following disciplines:
- Marketing – to guide the business and create the opportunity to make a sale.
- Development – to create necessary products to differentiate and satisfy the needs of the customer.
- Sales – to cause prospects to make a purchase decision in favor of your products.
- Operations – to provide the products on time, on quality, and on margin.
- IT – to improve internal and external operation execution and customer satisfaction.
- Finance – to provide guidance, general accounting, and risk management.

Experience and Capabilities

Remember the story of the engineer who became the marketing manager? Sounds funny, but it happens every day. Having the right talent, in the right position, at the right time, is critical to your success. Simply having a person with a business card that says "VP, Marketing" does your business no good, unless that same person truly has the needed experience and capabilities to match your company's needs.

Do They Have Proven Experience?

Titles do not prove experience; personnel may have titles, some for long periods of time, and never actually gain any real experience that is applicable to your needs. A person with five years experience as a vice president of marketing in a large company might have simply been a manager, supervising the people with the true talent. Left alone, this VP may be unable to provide any measurable marketing skills without his staff.

A person might also have simply been inept and yet held the position for a long time just because the company failed to remove him. The larger the company; the easier it is for people to hide. It is essential that you determine, through the interviewing process, what real experience the person has that applies directly to what you need. Do not trust resumes as more than a general guide.

Do They Have Proven Performance?

If a person truly has the experience in the area you need, how well has he performed over that time? Did he always perform at or above expectations? Did he regularly excel? Or did he continually fail until being removed?

For example, when considering sales people, the first thing you want to know is, in what percent of their years (as a sales person) have they met or exceeded their quota. You should be suspect of sales people who say they, "helped the company grow;" you are interested in sales people who say they attained or exceeded sales goals ninety percent or more of the time, regardless of how well the company did.

When it comes to the rest of the needed disciplines, the scenario is the same. Find out if each person has proven performance that you can verify.

Are They Matched to Your Needs?

Do you need seasoned veterans who can hit the ground running? Do you need someone with direct industry experience who brings a Rolodex® of contacts or an immediate understanding of your technology? Do you have time to train? Are you qualified to train? Do you need entrepreneurial self-starters or do you need folks who are more comfortable in a structured environment?

Are They Matched to Your Team?

Just because someone has great experience and solid performance does not mean he or she is an automatic match for your needs. Assembling a team that can excel while "playing well together" is an arduous process. Not only must you find team members with great experience and proven performance, all members must be a good fit for your needs. You must find people who have similar experiences, capabilities, goals, and business styles so that they can "play nice together in the same sandbox."

Using a professional sports team analogy, many teams have cut star players because they were simply too disruptive to the team. Teams often fail to reach their potential because they cannot perform well because of the disruptive nature of ill-matched players. I can tell you from experience, having stars who do not play well with others does not work, and the sooner you "cut them loose" and get the right person in that spot, the sooner you will start to improve.

Far too many managers hold onto employees with great individual talent and terrible team skills, thinking this option the best choice. It is not, and if you remember anything about building teams remember this quote: "*The needs of the many outweigh the needs of the few or the one.*"[25] Build teams that excel and win together; do not let "prima donnas" or ill-positioned personnel destroy your chance of success.

Proper Balance

Balanced input maximizes output. Having too much of one discipline and not enough of another is a recipe for disaster. Are you selling more than you can build? Are you building more than you are selling? Are you developing more than the market wants?

If you balance your disciplines, experience and capabilities, and the amount of each, you will build teams that perform smoothly, and cause your business to excel. Do not let budgets hold you back. Raise more money, get advisors or board members with the required talent, but get what you need and win!

Here is an exercise that will help you evaluate whether or not you have the right talent and balance.

1. Under Discipline, give yourself five points for every discipline for which your business has talent (person, contractor or vendor) clearly identified. Mark zero for every one you are missing.

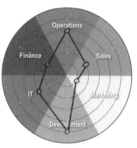

2. Under Capabilities & Experience, if you identified that you have talent that is clearly identified for a particular discipline, rate them on a scale from 0 to 5, relative to what their experience and capabilities are within that discipline, with 5 being the best.

3. Add your scores from both sections and put that total number where indicated. Total Score.

4. Using the grade chart provided, give yourself a final grade.

5. On the clean discipline wheel provided, using your pencil or pen, place a dot at the appropriate capability ring from the numbers you circled in Capabilities & Experience. If you said you did not have a discipline then place the dot on the zero.

6. Connect the dots to form a complete shape. (See example)

Discipline:
Sales: 0 or 5
Marketing: 0 or 5
Development: 0 or 5
Operations: 0 or 5
IT: 0 or 5
Finance: 0 or 5

Capability & Experience:
Sales: 0,1,2,3,4,5
Marketing: 0,1,2,3,4,5
Development: 0,1,2,3,4,5
Operations: 0,1,2,3,4,5
IT: 0,1,2,3,4,5
Finance: 0,1,2,3,4,5

Grade Scale:
55 – 60 = A
48 – 54 = B
42 – 47 = C
36 – 41 = D
< 36 = F

Total Score: _____

Grade: _____

When it comes to your grade, my experience would indicate that the average grade is "C" or lower, with very few "A" grades ever seen. Many people believe they have a stronger team than they actually do, and this exercise is designed to help you take a more objective look at your employees and at your ability to succeed.

When considering the shape created by your results, visualize that shape as a wheel. Now place four of them on your vehicle, and you will get an idea of the smoothness of your business ride. The smoother the circle; the smoother the ride. The larger the circle; the faster the ride. Ultimately remember, "*It is impossible to move fast if you can't move smoothly.*"

If your goal is to create a winning company, you will need to move smoothly and swiftly over a sustained period of time. You cannot create that momentum with a team that is out of balance. Having the right disciplines, with applicable experience and proven capabilities in proper balance, all matched to your needs, increases your odds of success and the ease and speed at which it can be achieved.

RECIPE CHECK: BALANCED TEAM

- Make sure you have all six disciplines involved in your business.
- Make sure each discipline is represented by talent who has the needed experience and capabilities.
- Make sure you have a balanced team that is matched to the business' needs and to each other.

Getting the Right Talent

It is one thing to agree that you need the right talent, in the right place, at the right time. It is another reality to actually get the job done.

First, you have to assess any talent you currently have. If the employees are not the right talent, you must be willing to replace them. Far too many companies simply will not eliminate weak or misplaced talent. Rather, they suffer along, continually trying to train or coach the person: "I gave them a tough review, let's give them another six months," or "They have so much experience, we can't afford to lose them."

An idea I have shared with developing leaders for my teams is this: When you release someone from a position for which he or she is not optimally suited, two things will always be true: (1) You will always wish you had done the termination sooner; and (2) you will never regret the decision.

Terminating or reclassifying personnel is a difficult part of the job. Yet, your responsibility is to create and to maintain a vital business to serve your customers and to foster a quality working environment for your employees. Allowing a single individual to jeopardize that responsibility is irrational, and not the action of a successful, respected leader.

When terminating or demoting individuals, if you conduct this action correctly, you will also provide great guidance to the person you are removing. You do an employee no service if you fail to provide honest reasons behind your action. Telling someone you are removing them because of cutbacks when it is not true, or any other fabricated reason, to soften the blow, is just trying to make your job easier. Tell the employee the truth in a respectful and legal manner, give him suggestions for his next opportunity, and be honest. You and the other person will be better for it.

How to Find Talent
When seeking talent, there are five key components to the process:
- Job descriptions
- Interviewing techniques
- Work environment
- Recruiting resources
- Screening processes

Job Descriptions

First and foremost, never decide to make a new hire or to start the interview process without first writing a complete job description. Poor or wrong hires are the most costly mistakes your business can make. Non-performance, negative impact to company morale, or damaging your company brand – all can occur by putting the wrong person in the wrong role.

Quality job descriptions help you understand your true business' needs, requiring that you analyze needs and write them down, rather than simply acting on impulse or emotion. A quality job description includes:

- A simple description of the position with the title and reporting structure:
  - Example: XYZ company is seeking an inside sales professional for the position of Sales Representative. This position reports directly to the company VP of Sales.
- Next, make a list of the essential functions, duties, and responsibilities, including how time should be spent on the job:
  - Example:
    - Sales-lead management in the company's customer relationship management (CRM) system – 10%
    - Telephone sales' prospecting and order generation – 50%
    - Follow-up on internet sales transactions – 20%
    - Order entry, order tracking, and customer follow-up - 20%
- Next, make a list of the performance requirements:
  - Example:
    - Sales revenue against quota
    - New business development

- On-time order delivery
- Customer retention
- Then, make a list of the skills, experience or other require-ments the candidate must have and those that would be nice to have. This is a critical area. Whatever qualities you list as "must have" criteria will become your minimum, under which you will NOT interview ANY candidates. You will tell all recruiting personnel of this decision and will make no exceptions.

There are far too many cases where exceptions were made to this approach because (A) you "liked" the person; (B) the person performed well in other roles and surely will adapt; or (C) you need someone now and do not have time to keep looking. When a recruiter says, "I know this candidate does not meet all your criteria, but we really like him," do not interview him. You will probably like the person as well, make a hire, and then in six months will be terminating the new employee because he did not have the needed criteria. Make your list of qualities and needs and hold to it; your business will be better for it.

- Finally, outline expected compensation. You must provide compensation and incentive programs that attract and re-tain the level of talent needed to attain your goals.

I know a sales executive for a well established business that has a group of direct sales representatives living across the country. He is relatively new to the position and has been tasked with significant and consistent revenue growth. The company, however, has a long standing policy of paying their sales representatives base salaries in the $50,000 / year range *with zero incentive compensation and no expense account for client entertainment. No matter how well the sales representative does, he or she will make the same amount every year. A person has no incentive to go beyond the basic expectation and has no ability to entertain new or existing prospects. As a result, this company has built a complacent selling organization staffed by mediocre talent. In this environment, the new sales executive has no ability to attract or retain higher quality sales talent or to motivate the talent he currently has to achieve greater performance. Growth is simply expected to occur based upon the "genius" of the products. Unfortunately, the ability to attain the requested revenue growth, under this type of program, will be nearly impossible.*

Quality job descriptions:
- Help you determine the real need for the hire
- Help you understand the required experience and capabilities
- Prepare you to make an objective, hiring decision
- Help you create the right expectations of the new hire
- Help the prospective hire to make a good decision, and once employed, to contribute more effectively
- Outline the compensation required to attract and retain the right candidates

Interviewing
Most interviews are conducted in a very informal manner, with no objective plan, and the decision is ultimately a product of emotion. Typical interviewers read a resume, put the text aside, ask a few general questions, allow the candidate to ask questions, and then hire the one, "they like."

To build a quality team, your interviewing process must

gather the right information and allow you to objectively compare one candidate to another, based upon company needs. You must ask all candidates the same list of questions and score all candidates objectively on their answers, as well as experience, capabilities, and "fit" in the company. If you have other personnel, advisors, or board members available to interview candidates you must involve the same people asking the same questions with each candidate. The result will provide objective and comparable information.

To assist the interview structure and to provide an objective scoring system, I suggest you use an interview questionnaire and a scoring template for each hired position. The example provided here is for a "Marketing Communications Director." The questions to ask all candidates are listed on the left. An area is provided for your notes, and there is a section for you to indicate a score, based upon the provided answer. There is also a section to indicate areas of concern for follow-up during the reference checking stage.

Interview Template

QUESTION	NOTES	SCORE 1-5
Overall presence and appearance		
Please describe marketing. What functions and responsibilities does it include?		
Please describe the role marketing should play in a business' overall direction.		
Please describe the role marketing should play in the selling process.		
Can you describe how brands are built as well as sustained?		

THE RECIPE FOR BUSINESS SUCCESS

What are the major challenges for marketing in today's environment?		
Please describe your experience in the following areas:		
Public presentations		
Traditional marketing communications		
Social marketing communications		
Conventions and trade shows		
Writing and editing		
Written planning		
Budget creation and management		
Market identification and validation		
Specific industry		
How would you describe your detail orientation?		
Please describe your performance at your past two positions; successes and failures.		
What type of leadership do you like best? Why?		
What are your strengths?		
What are your weaknesses?		
What are your five year goals and career goals?		
Why do you want this job?		
Also score on:		
Overall communication ability		
Portfolio review		
Screening / references		
Second interview		
Notes and areas of concern:		
	Total	

Obviously, scores will be somewhat subjective depending on the question asked. You will likely ask additional questions, based upon responses. If you create perceptive questions that cover required information to objectively compare candidates, this process will significantly improve the quality of your hires.

Make sure that if you involve other personnel, everyone uses the same questionnaire. You will then be able to objectively compare answers and have a meaningful discussion. Once all interviews are completed, the questionnaires will reveal the most qualified candidates and allow you to compare them more objectively.

When selecting a proper time to conduct interviews, the choice should not be whenever you can "squeeze it" in your schedule. If you arrange and conduct an interview while you are focused on a business issue, you will go through the mechanics and learn nothing. Your emotional outlook during a single interview, but not during others, will affect hiring. You should choose a time when you can give consistent, undivided, and non-stressed attention to the candidate and to the process.

Work Environment
The right work environment has everything to do with attracting the right talent, and it's not something you can fake. Company environments (cultures) become well known in the hiring community. If you use the terms "entrepreneurial" and "empowering" to describe the work environment in your recruitment process, you want to make sure that it's true. If not, good prospects will already know. Those who do not might be attracted by what you say, but if you hire them, they will quickly become dis-

enchanted with your company and will not stay. You will lose the time and money invested in that person; your business will be further compromised by grumblings of a disgruntled employee.

The vitality of your company also becomes well known. If you have a financially sound, growing business, it is easier to hire great talent. If you are on the verge of collapse, it will not be so easy.

One of the truths about hiring is that you cannot effectively secure and retain talent that is at odds with your environment. If the atmosphere is autocratic and process driven, you will attract talent that is compliant, tends to require direction, prefers structure and does not often step "outside the box." If your environment is entrepreneurial, celebrates mistakes as learning experiences, rewards risk taking, and, perhaps provides too much autonomy, then you will attract talent that consistently challenges the status-quo, is self-structured, and lives "outside the box."

Consider the type of work environment you create. It will have an impact on the talent you can attract and retain. If you will have a regular need for high-quality talent, then you must become a preferred employer. Be a company that everyone in the area, or industry, wants to work for because of your culture, your benefits, the quality of your team, the performance of your business, or in essence – your environment.

As part of creating a great culture, share successes, provide rewards, and create programs that continually drive and motivate performance. Examples I have used include:

- To celebrate excellent business performance, offer impromptu award bonuses or things as simple as May Day baskets with $100 bills in them. These gestures go a long way to say "thank you" to everyone. Make it a practice to give such items to all employees, including temporary employees, and you will never have trouble finding temps in the future. I remember handing a $1,000+ check to a temporary production worker on her first day.

- To help the operations team increase productivity and not drive up overhead cost, we hired a company valet who would handle their personal errands - laundry, groceries, take-out meals, anything that did not entail transporting people or pets. This service allowed people to earn over-time and get to their errands accomplished. The company increased output in an efficient manner, and the service attracted new talent when needed.

A final thought on company environment is the "on-boarding" process you use when bringing in new team members. Do you simply push them into the job, or do you professionally acclimate them to the business and the team. Do you have an "on-boarding" process that you follow for every new hire that maximizes initial productivity, as well as the positive experience of the hire? Things to consider in this plan include:

- Relocating employees need help with:
  - Real Estate
  - Community infrastructure
  - Education / schools
- Review of the job description, including its responsibilities and measurements.
- Introduction to all pertinent team members and their roles.
- Facility and resource tour.
- Review of the employee manual (benefits, dress code, hours of operation, holidays, etc.).
- Generally accepted rules and procedures (the way you do

business) including a review of your corporate culture.

If you maximize this initial experience, you will create a better hiring environment and the quality of team member you can attract.

Recruiting Resources

There are a number of resources you can employ when recruiting talent, and it is likely that you will need to use more than one in order to assemble a solid talent pool.

Typical resources include:

- Recruiters: When using recruiters, pay careful attention to securing those who specialize in the type of talent sought. Like most quality service providers, recruiters have areas of focus and strength. Determine when it is applicable to use one, exclusive recruiter or multiple recruiters. Typically, this decision is based upon the time you have to generate a quality number of candidates, the geography you need to cover, and the proven expertise of the recruiter. Remember, a "headhunter" works for you, and must provide the value required.
- Employee referrals: Get your team involved and have them provide candidate referrals. If they like your environment, they will be happy to refer others. Consider paying a referral fee if the candidate is hired.
- Vendor referrals: Get your vendors involved. In many cases, they are aware of candidates from within your industry who would be ideal. If you do not ask, you will not learn about these possibilities.
- Websites: There are a number of job sites you can consult. A few of the most popular national job sites include Monster, Careerbuilder, Dice, and Hotjobs.[26] There are also lo-

cal sites, regional sites, and trade association sites. You can also search Google® to help you locate many other options.

- Social media; Linkedin®, Twitter®, Facebook®, etc., provide you instant access to a wide audience at nearly no cost.[27]
- Newspapers and industry journals provide classic paths to placing candidate searches and locating job-seekers.

Just like advertising and prospecting for customers, your plan for attracting the right candidates requires a strategic mix of all these options. If you take the process seriously, you will generate a quality list of candidates from which to select your next team members.

Screening

Making a hiring decision based upon a resume and two or three hours of interviewing is still very risky. To make better decisions, add additional screening tools and procedures to your qualification process, and your hiring success will improve significantly.

Options include:

- References: It is always important to check a candidate's references, but the most non-productive thing you can do is to simply call the persons provided by the candidate and say, "How did you like Bill?" First, if the candidate is savvy, the reference is prepped to say, "I loved Bill." If you are going to call references, the first thing to do is to prepare a list of questions, that you will ask, based upon what you have learned in the interview(s).

By this point, you should have specific questions or concerns you would like to address. When you have a reference on the phone, ask questions like this: "If you were to score Bill on a scale of 1-5 in the area of leadership, what score would you give him?" When the reference gives you a number (say three), you can reply "That's interesting. Why did you score him a three instead of a five? Here the reference must: (A) rate the candidate for you; and (B) give you additional, specific answers based upon his experience with the candidate.

If you employ this method, you will learn much about the candidate in a very short time. Remember, not all references will give you information other than what their legal counsel told them to supply - name and time employed. If this is the case, simply thank them for their time and move on to another reference.

- Involving your team in the interview process, using additional team members to separately interview candidates, adds objectivity. Be consistent and use the same individuals for each candidate. If you are interviewing for a key executive position, you may consider having the final candidates make a presentation to your entire leadership team as to why they are best suited for the job. In my experience, when you are hiring a senior executive, it is good to involve their peer group in the process so there is team acceptance, and the new hire is welcomed.
- Assessment tests / profiles: There are a number of screening and pre-hiring tools that assess everything from ability and skills to reliability and work ethic, integrity, and

personality. Some of the most popular include the DISC assessment, Myers-Briggs Type Indicator (MBTI), and the Caliper Profile.[28] There are also a number of resources to help you prepare for the interview, conduct background checks, rate candidates, make an offer, and create a formal orientation program.

I have been a twenty-year user and advocate of the Caliper Profile. This program has helped me hire countless sales representatives, senior executives, and other team members. I have found its results to be accurate and consistent, and when I have made hiring decisions in opposition to its results, I have always found that I should have listened.

Regardless of the screening product you choose to use, you must use the tool consistently for it to become a quality component of your hiring process. You must also get proper, legal counsel to explain how it can be used in the decision process.[29]

Look to the following web sites for multiple screening options:
a. Wonderlic (http://www.wonderlic.com)
b. Profiles International (http://www.profilesinternational.com)
c. The Myers & Briggs Foundation (http://www.myersbriggs.org)
d. Brainbench (http://www.brainbench.com)
e. Caliper Profile (http://www.calipercorp.com)
f. DISC (http://www.disctest.com)

RECIPE CHECK: BALANCED TEAM

- Always begin with a complete job description.
- Employ effective and consistent interviewing techniques.
- Create a work environment to attract the talent you need.
- Use recruiting resources to maximize qualified options.
- Employ multiple screening processes to improve your success rate.

Team Summary

If you build a team with balanced disciplines, experience, capabilities, goals, and individuals who can work well on the same team, your business success will improve significantly. If you tolerate imbalance in your team, you will significantly impact your overall business "Recipe," and will reap the rewards accordingly. Build a great team – your success depends on it!

SCORE YOUR BUSINESS

At this point, take a moment and score your business on page 185. If you can truly say that you have a talented and balanced team as outlined, score yourself at ten. If you can identify some of the disciplines, capabilities, and experience but still need to secure or develop others, score yourself accordingly. Your scoring will allow you to identify opportunities for improved performance, so grade yourself honestly.

LEADERSHIP
The Critical Role it Plays in Success

Leadership is the ability to build, develop, and motivate a team of diverse, talented individuals to effectively attain common goals. Sounds easy, but there are many challenges. Missed opportunities, poor performance, wrong or poor talent, bad environments, high employee turnover, and lack of growth – all are problems created by the lack of effective leadership.

Absolutely critical to maximizing the success of any business is the guidance provided by quality leadership. Poor or inappropriate guidance results in poor or limited results. Like all other ingredient and execution components, you can have all of the essentials and still fail without this one.

I have watched numerous businesses, all with great promise, fail to reach even a portion of their potential because of poor leadership. Did the companies think they had poor leadership? Of course not; those who run the ship must be great leaders, right? If a leader is not succeeding or not reaching higher potentials, it is not his fault. Blame falls to the staff, the market, the competition, or the environment.

There are billion-dollar businesses that should be multi-billion dollar companies; the only thing standing in the way is better leadership. Many will read this book and get great value out of all the other chapters. However, when arriving here, they will conclude that they are a leader. In reality, the reader is not and will completely minimize the learning process.

Leadership is not about seniority, intelligence, or who

owns the business. It is not about age, net worth, or family name. Leadership is not about the ability to command. Leadership is about the ability to maximize business results through the collective capabilities of a diverse team.

Clearly there is a difference between being "in charge" and "leading." Experience and history indicates that most in-charge positions are staffed by managers, not leaders. In the late 1980s, I found a description of the difference between leaders and managers in Fortune® Magazine. I typed it, framed it, and the text has hung in my office since that day as a constant reminder and self assessment tool.

I have modified the article's list a bit over time:

Managers administer and maintain
> **Leaders innovate and develop**

Managers rely on processes and controls
> **Leaders rely on people and trust**

Managers seek compliance and guide in their own image
> **Leaders seek results through the collective capabilities of their team**

Managers do things right
> **Leaders do the right thing**

Managers administer and maintain corporate policy, programs and procedures. They follow a status quo because that is expected. They rely on processes, systems, and controls as mechanisms to get things done. How things are done is as important as the desired result. In many cases, it is acceptable to fail, if you used the right procedure.

Managers guide in their own image and seek compliance. "If you would just do it my way, we would be more successful," is their mantra. They suppress challenge and creative thinking. Ironically, employees who get promoted in this type of environment are, in many cases, those that comply and conform to the manager's desires. Those that challenge the norm are seen as disruptive, kept back, or terminated. In the process, some of the best leaders and creative talent are removed from an organization as compliance and bureaucracy is built.

As a relatively new director-level executive in a Fortune 500 company, I was asked by the CEO how they could attract more people like me. I was someone who always challenged the status-quo and constantly looked for new ways to grow faster or build better teams. My response was fast and simple, "Stop suppressing people like me for that quality." In that company, like many others, challenging the established culture, processes, and controls was simply not tolerated.

Managers install processes and systems to improve internal accountability and replication, many times at the expense of customer deliverables and creative expansion. Managers see employees as tools to be used to improve their personal success.

Leaders, on the other hand, have a significant disdain for managers and the resulting culture. Leaders innovate and develop constantly, always looking for new ways to attain better results. Leaders are results oriented and shun processes that do not add value to the customer. They rely on people and trust, rather than procedures and controls. Process and procedure are tools to be used and modified to attain results. If new outcomes are needed, processes change immediately; trust is placed in people driving the process, not the reverse.

Leaders understand that if you keep adding new process and new controls on top of existing structure, you end up with a bureaucratic organization that has lost all the flexibility and talent needed to maximize results.

Results are Reflective

The average employee of any organization wants to do a good job. He wants to be appreciated, have fun, grow, and learn. He comes to work with ideas and excitement. Yet, in many organizations, these things are suppressed and the value that could have been realized from that employee is minimized. There is a clear difference in organization culture run by a manager versus a leader.

In manager-run organizations, employees tend to perform as asked, putting in their eight hours and no more. If the boss is an ego maniac and oppressor of individuality, the employees spend time complaining or gossiping about the manager and the environment. All of us can relate to one or more experiences with that type of culture.

In such acidic environments, part of an employee's day is made up of gossip-level discussions, resulting in less than eight hours of work. Hours spent working are clearly not as productive as they could be. On some days, you might get less than 50% of an employee's maximum output, forcing the need for more employees per task. The more oppressive the culture; the most costly the overhead.

In leader driven organizations employees love their jobs. They come in early, stay late, skip breaks, and work through lunch, all because they want to do so. They know such commitment is not required, but they want to see the business excel, and they want to be part of the success. In this type of organization, employees produce at levels above 100%, and the output is indicative of their loyalty and enthusiasm. If you want your business to attain the maximum possible results, it is absolutely essential to harness the maximum power of each person working on your team.

Typical Leadership Traits
In years of studying, I have assembled a list of traits gleaned from different sources and experiences that I believe define true leadership.

Leaders know that company principles and the resulting culture mean everything. In Lou Gerstner's book <u>Who Says Elephants Can't Dance</u>[30] – the story of his time at IBM, Mr. Gerstner says, "*I came to see, in my time at IBM, that culture isn't just one aspect of the game – it is the game. In the end, an organization is nothing more than the collective capacity of its people to create value.*" I have never seen a better description of the impact of culture on a business. If you want to learn what the debilitating effects of a highly bureaucratic organization look like, and what efforts are required to change it, the book is highly recommended.

At age sixteen, Berkley Bedell started selling hand-tied flies to fishing tackle shops and vacationing anglers. After he completed college, he started Berkley® and Company, which focused on cable wire fishing leaders. The Iowa-based company did very well, selling a top-notch product and having an excellent reputation. Dealers, customers, and employees liked working with Bedell and the business he had created.

When he decided to run for public office (United States Representative), Bedell wanted the business to continue and he hired an MBA graduate to run the company. This new person completely changed the business culture, implementing process management strategies to improve bottom line performance. He flipped the culture, changing from a customer and employee-focused organization to a corporation focused primarily on shareholder value and net profit. In just three years, the company nearly failed. Good people left; sales slowed, and Bedell's business, one he had built from scratch, was headed for the history books.

Bedell asked his son, Tom, an accomplished entrepreneur, who was running a political campaign consulting business at the time, to take a look at the business. If something was not done, the business was going to fail. Tom spent time with the employees, got on a plane, and then met personally with the company's top distributors. They provided much feedback about how things used to be and what they had come to expect from Berkley. They also told him how things had changed; Tom asked for three months to devise a plan on fixing the business before making any decision to switch to another supplier.

Tom Bedell went back and assumed the position as CEO. He gathered all the top managers and reminded them that they were the team who had built the company's original culture. He acknowledged that somewhere along the way, the culture had been lost, and they needed to get it back. He informed the management team that they needed to make a decision. Did they want to rebuild the old culture and stay with the company or would they rather take a severance package and leave?

Tom Bedell revitalized the business by reestablishing its original culture. The company grew tremendously, merged with multiple complimentary entities, and eventually evolved into a $300+ million company Pure Fishing® (http://www. purefishing.com).[31]

Leaders provide vision and focus. They see where they want to go and set the direction accordingly. They communicate direction, clearly, often and consistently. They do not waver. Leaders keep the entire team on focus and on track. They reduce roadblocks for their team so that they can execute better and faster. Leaders never become the barrier. Leaders focus on strategy, not tactics.

Leaders know that people are the most important resource. They know that people create their best intellectual property and market differentiation. Show me a patent, and I will show you the people who created it, and the people who can design around it. I have been a part of securing many significant business deals around the world in my career. From my experience, as I was sitting in boardrooms of small and large corporations, in every case, it was the team that got the work done. The people on the team who wanted success would make it happen.

Leaders know that work enjoyment and company performance are closely linked. Happy employees are productive because they want to be, not because they must. Happy employees are far more willing to contribute the extra effort needed to excel.

Leaders know that people are individuals. Every person is different - wants, life goals, family situation. What motivates each person is different. If you want the most from every person on your team, you need to consider each one individually. It may be that the best person for a particular role needs flexible work hours, a different working environment, or an alternative compensation structure. I have been fortunate to work with a significant number of great people in my career, all very strong individuals. Each person had great skills, and with those skills came individuality.

I had a CTO (Chief Technology Officer) on one of my teams who was the most gifted computer technologist that I have ever met. No matter the corporate location, no matter the company engineering talent, this person was technically stronger and, most importantly, was able to modify his language and communicate at any level needed to convey value. From helping each client better understand how to improve his own products, to assisting our internal team in solving a client's needs, this person was responsible for a significant part of our global brand and related success.

However, this gifted CTO had a few idiosyncrasies that drove some team members crazy. He worked late into the night, was never in the office before 9:00 or 9:30 AM, and was not available for early meetings. If he did attend, he was sleepy, had a bowl of cereal in his hand, and his brain was only partially engaged. His office looked like the victim of a typhoon - piles of papers everywhere with no apparent organization. One night, I got a call from the police department to say that our building was open and one office had been ransacked. I said, "let me guess which one," and then described it. We had a good laugh; I went over and locked the door. This same person also had problems with schedules and timelines.

On more than one occasion, I had people in my office asking me to "make him comply," to make him more like them. What was very clear, as is true with most everyone, was that the CTO was not going to change his fundamental style. If we wanted the huge value he provided, we would also need to organize around his style. Not everyone liked this adjustment, but it worked, and the company was better for adjusting. And all of those employees who did or did not agree with that plan had idiosyncrasies that we also absorbed, including my own.

Leaders put trust in people over processes. People create results. If those results require specific processes, then good people can put them in place and change them as needed. I have no issue with processes. That being said, the only rule I have is, at no time will any business I am leading put in processes, procedures or controls that do not add direct value to the end customer. At no time will we put in bureaucracy that *reduces* value to our customers. From my perspective, it is impossible to create processes that can in any way make up for, or replace the need for, great talent.

Leaders celebrate mistakes. I have had many experiences with executives who are autocratic, caustic and oppressive. In these organizations, when an employee makes a mistake that costs the company money or damages a customer relationship, executives hunt down the worker and strip him down.

If you have an organization where everyone is happy and focused on success, when an employee makes a mistake, he or she feels terrible about the outcome. People who care about their work denigrate themselves; they are embarrassed around peers, and in many cases, the role of the leader is to minimize the pain. Mistakes are learning experiences. If you are not making mistakes, you are not trying hard enough and are not learning. If you celebrate mistakes, you foster risk-taking and individual growth; your organization will grow from it. There is a quote from one of the founders of Google® that makes the same point.

Sheryl Sandberg, a former vice president in charge of the company's automated advertising system, committed an error that cost Google several million dollars. When she realized the magnitude of her mistake, she went to inform Larry Page, Google's co-founder and unofficial thought leader. "God, I feel really bad about this," Sandberg told Page, who accepted her apology. As she turned to leave, Page said, "I'm so glad you made this mistake, because I want to run a company where we are moving too quickly and doing too much, not being too cautious and doing too little. If we don't have any of these mistakes, we're just not taking enough risk."[32] This is leadership.

Leaders know that customers are the company's lifeblood. They stay involved with customers and listen to them regularly. Leaders never get "beyond" or "above" talking to customers. Leaders support their customers with every resource and build a company culture that rewards unwavering support to them.

In the 90's there was a television commercial that showed a CEO in the board room passing out airline tickets to all the company executives. As he was distributing them, he said roughly, "I got a call today from a long-time customer. Seems we have grown out of touch with his needs in favor of our own. As such, all of us are going to get on the plane and visit all of our key customers and get back in touch." Now clearly this was aimed at selling airline tickets, but the underlying message is hugely applicable – think about it.

Leaders surround themselves with talent. Leaders understand their own weaknesses and build talent around them. This means that they have to acknowledge that they have weaknesses. Leaders know they do; managers believe they do not. Leaders know their success is in the hands of their team. They never try to know everything and are comfortable relying on their teams. When I ask a question that pertains to their area of responsibility and they confidently say, "I don't know, but I can find out. When would you like the answer?" When they can do that without feeling diminished for not knowing the answer themselves, they are starting to lead.

Leaders hire people who are better in specific disciplines and delegate the company's success to them. Theodore Roosevelt said, *"The best executive is the one who has the sense enough to pick good men to do what he wants done, and the self-restraint enough to keep from meddling with them while they do it."* (Chase Sargent, <u>From Buddy to Boss</u>)[33]

Leaders listen to, and seek challenge from their team. Leaders understand that challenge and debate from and within their team results in better overall decisions. Leaders do not like to make decisions in a vacuum; they seek out challenges and modify decisions accordingly. If a member of your team comes into your office and says (in a respectful manner), "I disagree with something," how do you react? A leader says "That's interesting; can you tell me why?" He then asks, "Can you give me a better solution" or, "Can you explain your position?" If the team member presents a case that makes sense, and collectively, a decision process is modified accordingly, the company wins and more team members are likely to voice their ideas. Enhanced business performance is directly related to better decision making.

The ideas and frustrations you want to hear are those expounded by an employee to his or her spouse over dinner. The very best, most creative ideas and the root causes of poor performance or poor employee morale go home with your staff every day. The real key is to create a culture where those frustrations and ideas are heard and acted upon at work. I have worked in environments where challenge is seen as disrespect and even insubordination. These same organizations are worse for the environment they create, whether they think so or not.

Leaders understand the dynamics of high-performance teams. Leading high-performance teams requires a significant amount of flexibility and tolerance for individuality. Highly-driven, highly-talented people tend to continually challenge the status quo. They challenge their leadership, staff, and peers.

The leader's job is to keep them on focus and to channel their talent and energy toward a common goal, maximizing results and minimizing consternation. High-performance teams can be disruptive; they create competition among their peers. They degrade others and create untenable situations to the point where one or more of your most talented folks may simply leave.

As a part of an Inc. Magazine program, I attended a meeting with a group of other multiple-year, Inc. 500 winning CEOs. Many of them complained about having to spend time keeping personnel on track - keeping them from "killing" each other. My thought was, the real job of a leader in a fast growing organization is to *assemble* and *develop* the team needed to win. This, in and of itself, might absorb up to 50% of a leader's time and should be the leader's primary job. Actual business operations are the responsibility of the team.

In baseball, it is the head coach's job to win from the dugout. He has to win without playing a position on the field. He has to deal with all kinds of personalities and get them to execute together as a team. That is the true job of the leader.

Leaders cause decisions to be made. Leaders know that lack of decision making is detrimental to success. They gather enough data (but not "all" the data) to make good decisions, and they make them in a timely fashion. Leaders seek consensus in decision making to improve execution. Through team challenge, leaders gain valuable information that makes decisions faster and better; in the process, they gain the needed consensus to execute effectively.

Leaders act in the absence of consensus because it not always possible to gain it and waiting can be costly. Leaders know that making "no decision" is always the wrong decision. Nothing frustrates team members more than a leader who cannot make a decision. If you make a wrong decision, take responsibility, learn from the result, and make a new decision.

Leaders treasure reputation. They treasure the reputation of their company, their team, and their products. They understand that their personal image is secondary and is truly based upon the success of their company and team. Leaders do not take accolades for their business success; they pass it on to their team. If you read an interview with a CEO where responses start with "I" instead of "we" and the quoted content is about him or her rather than the team, then you are not reading about a leader.

This last year, my parents presented me with a very special Christmas present. It was an album with media clippings from nearly thirty years of my business career. Included were promotions, new jobs, business successes, awards, and speaking engagements. As I read through them, besides being envious of how young I used to look, I was proud to discover that in nearly all of the articles on business success, my quotes were focused on success being the direct result of a team. Leaders earn their reputation through the performance of others.

Leaders know that teams follow out of respect and desire, not fear of retribution. True leaders inspire their teams to want success as badly as they do. Their teams help to achieve goals because they want to do so. You cannot force employees into excellence; they must arrive there on their own.

Leaders know that respect is earned, not appointed by job title. You cannot be promoted into leadership; you earn it by consistent, trusted performance. You set an example for others to follow. In many companies, the person with the highest title is not the one leading.

Earlier in my career, in a 500-person organization where I was responsible for sales, marketing, and customer support, the company distributed a survey to all employees for checking on morale and to better understand how to improve as an organization. One of the questions asked employees, "who was leading the company?" Who was providing its direction? Both myself and the CFO, with whom I worked very closely and I remain friends with today, had the most responses because we were perceived as leading the organization. That CFO taught me the core implications of finance on an orga-

nization, and although I fought it, I remain forever in his debt for this education. In turn, he might say that I taught him a bit about sales and marketing.

Leaders provide passion. They serve as the company cheerleader, are excited about company direction, work long hours alongside their teams, set excellent examples, are active and accessible, are driven, and embody the true spirit of the organization. If leaders are excited, happy, and motivated, so will their team. The reverse is also true.

Leaders have a strong sense of self and are not easily influenced by popularity. Leaders are driven to succeed, and in many cases, that means going against what might be popular or acceptable. They do not try to be "friends" with their team and they do not make decisions based upon friendship. On any given day, someone in the organization will be unhappy with something. A leader knows his job is to guide a team to success. Many times in the process only a leader will be able to see the overall effects of each person's value. They truly understand the old phrase, "It's lonely at the top."

Leaders are secure individuals, and although they tend to have strong egos that are fueled by success, such is not required to maintain purpose.

Leaders know that the capability to lead comes from desire, self analysis and hard work. If you want to be a quality leader, success is not about what you read or what you study. It is what you learn and convert to practice. Like all disciplines (business, sports, or entertainment), you can only excel at leadership if you practice and employ it.

On your way home from work, every day, ask yourself, "What did I do today that was leader-like?" Ask, "What did I do today that was more like a manager?" If you honestly review each day in that manner, and on the following day, if you correct the manager-like mistakes by making apologies or changing decisions, your leadership skills and overall performance will improve. Respect in you will grow, and you will feel the difference. All leaders and managers make mistakes, but it is the leaders that admit them and correct them.

The Leadership Test

Shown is a leadership self test by A. J. Schuler, a renowned expert on leadership and team performance.[34] Take the time right now to find out whether or not you possess the characteristics of a true leader. Below the test are answers that indicate whether your response is more like that of a leader or a manager.

	TRUE	FALSE
I think more about immediate results than I do about mentoring others.	❏	❏
People will be motivated if you pay them enough.	❏	❏
It's nice to know about people's long-term goals, but not necessary to get the job done.	❏	❏
If you have a consistent recognition system that rewards everyone in the same way, then that is enough.	❏	❏
The best way to build a team is to set a group goal that is highly challenging, maybe even "crazy."	❏	❏
My greatest pleasure in my job comes from making the work process more effective.	❏	❏
I spend more of my time and attention on my weaker performers than I do on my top performers, who basically take care of themselves.	❏	❏
It's better not to know anything about the personal lives and interests of the people who report to me.	❏	❏

Sometimes, it's almost as if I'm a "collector of people" because I'm always recruiting and getting to know new people.	❏	❏
I like to surround myself with people who are better at what they do than I am.	❏	❏
I am a lifelong student of what makes other people tick.	❏	❏
People talk about "mission" too much – it's best just to let people do their work and not try to bring values into the conversation.	❏	❏
It's my job to know everything that goes on in my area.	❏	❏
I pay close attention to how and where I spend my time, because the priorities I put into action are the ones that other people will observe and follow.	❏	❏
I've worked hard to get along with or understand people who are very different from me.	❏	❏

Leaders would most likely respond: F,F,F,F,T,F,F,F,T,T,T,F,F,T,T

Managers would most likely respond: T,T,T,T,F,T,T,T,F,F,F,T,T,F,F

(Link to expanded answers in the Supplement)

RECIPE CHECK: LEADERSHIP

If you want your business to reach its potential, it is essential that your business be run by a leader, not a manager. If that person is not you, find one; vest them in the success of the business, give them the responsibility, authority and tools to succeed, ask them what role you should play and get out of their way.

If, on the other hand, your goal is to have the top title, then get an outside mentor or coach that will honestly help you improve your leadership capabilities and do the hard work to improve. All of the other ingredients and execution requirements in this book rely on this capability.

SCORE YOUR BUSINESS

At this point – take a moment and score your business on page 185. If you can truly say that you have, or are, a leader as outlined herein, score yourself at ten. If you can identify some of the traits, but still need to work on others, score yourself accordingly. If you simply are not a leader, and you do not have one, score yourself a zero. Your scoring will allow you to identify opportunities for improved performance, so grade yourself honestly.

RESOURCES
Maximizing Execution Success

All of the planning done to this point has provided the ability to accurately create your financial plan and determine the needed resources. If you started here, you are doing the process backwards. If you start your planning by figuring how much overhead you have (or will have) and how much profit you want to make, and then back your way into the sales revenue and pricing structure, you are inviting failure.

The key to getting the "Recipe" right is to understand all that we have previously discussed and to then assemble the necessary resources. A successful business "Recipe" is contingent on multiple resources. The most obvious one is money, from which the balance of the resources can be generated. Also critical to your company are the right technical, human, information, and environmental resources.

Information Resources
It is impossible to maximize business success without accurate information to make good, strategic decisions. Successful businesses generate data and use it on a regular basis. Key documentation includes:

- Business performance data, which should be reviewed monthly, no later than the fifth or sixth of the month. If you wait until well into the following month and find an issue, you will have two months of impact before you can react. If your bank statements are restricting activity, roll up preliminary statements. At a minimum, you should be reviewing:

- Monthly income, cash flow, and balance sheets to monitor overall performance against plan, as well as to identify specific issues and opportunities. You should engage all department managers who have budget responsibility in this process so that they: (a) understand how their department impacts the overall performance of the business; and (b) so that they work as a team to execute the plan.

- Monthly revenue and gross margin by product line (group), to monitor performance to plan in both revenue and contribution margins. This check will help quickly identify market adoption, as well as production issues and opportunities. This analysis will also help identify products that should be promoted differently and identify specific production or procurement issues that need to be addressed.

- Monthly revenue and gross margin by customer (if applicable), to monitor pricing and the resulting contribution margin created by each customer. This process will help to identify the desired type of customer and those not actively sought. In addition, you will be able to identify sales personnel who negotiate more on price, and it will help you more effectively focus the business' marketing efforts.

• Economic impact data is information regarding the overall economy, including global, national, regional, and industry-specific items. Pay attention to current trends and forecasts to make sure that you are planning applicable impact within your monthly and quarterly review process.

- Competitive information includes the financial, product and marketing performance of your competitors; the data allows you to make better decisions in your monthly and quarterly reviews. Do not wait until your annual planning process to be assessing your competition; pay attention to them at all times.

- Technology information is essential. What technological advancements will impact your products, manufacturing processes, or IT capabilities? If you are aware of emerging trends, you can implement prior to the competition, improve operational efficiencies, and avoid being burdened with inappropriate amounts of obsolete inventory.

Technical Resources

Having the right technology balanced to your needs and abilities will provide optimal and efficient delivery of your products and services. There is a fine line between having more than you need and not having enough when it comes to technology. Similarly, if you are a roofer and still driving nails by hand, your labor could be lower and your productivity higher with the adoption of pneumatic tools.

Working with obsolete technology can reduce efficiencies, increase service expenses, impact order fulfillment, and diminish your competitive position. Having more technology than you need, especially at budget expenses that could be better invested in other areas of the business, is just as great a problem. For every business component, you need to analyze the available tools versus the rewards; make quality decisions that fit your ability to invest.

Human Resources

Arguably, your employees and contractors are your most valuable resources. Building a plan that takes excellent care of the people and contacts you have, and one that helps you to add the best personnel going forward, will be one of the most important steps in your success. If you take the time to write a plan to recruit, reward, and retain the team you need to excel, your business will be better for it.

Personnel items to consider and plan for:
- Assessing and matching talent to needs
- Recruiting partners and processes
- Compensation and incentive programs
- Performance evaluations
- Continued education
- Stock option programs
- Team-building events
- Benefits

Environmental Resources

The environment in which you and your team work can be critical to your success.
- Do you have an environment that respects privacy and maximizes productivity? People respect the ability to have some level of privacy. Do not assume that all people work well in the same environment; some employees are far more distracted than others, and, some need greater degrees of privacy or quiet to be productive. Good screening techniques will help you better understand individual, employee needs.

- Does your environment foster teamwork? Keep in mind

that teamwork comes from a culture that is inclusive and rewarding. Pay particular attention to not creating "walls" or "class" structure that creates resentment. On the other hand, do not assume that putting everyone out in an open room together is best for teamwork.

- Is your facility clean and well organized? People tend to emulate their environment, and untended facilities can create sloppy input and output. Create an environment that fosters respect for your building or office as well as those in it. Keep all staff areas clean and in good repair. Although this may sound minor or obvious, out of the thousands of businesses I have visited over the years, amazing differences were witnessed. *Once I made a presentation to the senior management of a major telecom provider. In the conference room was garbage from previous meetings, including half-full coffee cups with mold in them on the window ledges. As it was later revealed, working with this company proved to be indicative of that environment – sloppy and unprofessional.* Dress your business for success, because whether it is customers, employees, or vendors, your facility should shout your brand from the moment anyone enters.

- Is your location correct? Have you chosen expensive, high-traffic real estate for a business that does not need it? If so, you are wasting valuable capital. Have you chosen a less expensive, hard to find, low traffic location to save money when you actually need the opposite? In this case you will likely spend more money advertising to get the needed traffic than you would have spent on the right location in the first place.

Financial Resources

Securing third-party funding, like everything else we have discussed, is a process that requires expert preparation and execution. Whether you need start-up capital, capital to fund expanding operations, or acquisition capital, if you need other people's money to grow your business, you need to be prepared.

The first thing to remember when seeking funding sources is that you are, for all intents and purposes, selling the outside party on your business "Recipe." The better job that you do of supporting this vision, the easier and less expensive the money will be to secure.

If you look at the graphic on the cover of this book, you will note that the green block is at the top of the stairs. That representation means you need to climb the first four stairs to get to that position. If you have a strong "Strategic Fit," a solid and believable business plan, an experienced and balanced team, and a proven leader, you will find funding reasonably straight forward.

If, on the other hand, you are trying to skip stairs and jump to the funding level without some or all of the first four "Recipe" requirements, you will find your funding options as being limited to non-existent. A large number of businesses blame banks or investors for their inability to secure needed capital for growing or staying in business when they clearly do not have a "Recipe" that justifies the investment.

It is your job to lead your business to secure required funding. It is your job to understand what type of funding is best for your business. It is also your responsibility to determine what you need to do to secure that funding. Finally, your role requires making the presentation and sale. When securing debt, the best rates are available for the lowest risk account. When selling equity, the best valuations are available to the lowest risk opportunities.

There are multiple personalities within each type of funding resource. From banks to venture capitalists, you need to research individual institutions and the people you will be approaching and understand how your request will fit their lending or investment profile. In my experience, significant time is wasted making presentations to resources who simply do not take the level of required risk or who do not invest in the targeted industry or product. Do your homework and present the right opportunities to the right audience.

Always keep in mind that banks and investors are *for-profit organizations* or individuals. They are focused on one thing—making money with their money. The amount of risk they are willing to take is in direct relation to your cost of that same money. Banks take lower levels of risk, investors take significantly more, and the cost of the money is reflected accordingly. If you want the most options and the best deals, you need to build an excellent "Recipe" and make a persuasive case.

In this section you should outline:

- Needed funding. If your statements indicate that you will have negative cash flow months, outline the maximum amount of money needed, along with when the capital is needed. Remember that you should plan for at least 125% of what your projections indicate to cover unforeseen impacts.
- Use of funds. List the specific use of the funding required:
  - To fund operations:
    - Inventory, receivables, development, personnel, advertising, start-up costs, etc.

- To fund capital purchases:
  - Building, equipment, etc.

- Funding sources. Depending on the amount of needed funding and the overall capability of your business to secure different types of funding, outline the specific sources (and amounts) from which you plan to secure the needed maximum. When you make this list, be realistic. Do not indicate that you are going to get a $1 million bank loan if you have no business or personal collateral and no profit history.

  Sources include (but are not limited to):
  - Debt funding. Borrowing money on a note payable for a specific interest amount. There are multiple ways to debt fund your business, including:
    - Bank or similar lending institution:
      - Term notes. These are lump sums you borrow for a specific period and interest rate, typically two to five years, and are generally tied to specific assets. Not designed for working capital, these loans normally require interest and principal payments to amortize the loan by maturity, but there are many other variations.
      - Lines of Credit (LOC). Loan amounts for which you qualify, but take in increments and pay down in increments. Typically called floating or revolving LOC's, these types of notes are generally used to offset cash required to fund inventory and accounts receivables, i.e. working capital. The amount you can borrow is typically tied to inventory and accounts receivables, creating a

floating borrowing base.

You can typically borrow 50% on inventory, not including WIP (work in process), obsolete or slow moving items. You may receive 70%-80% on receivables, not including those over ninety days old or invoices to accounts in other countries.
- Investor secured notes (below).

- Investor debt instruments:
  - High interest loans with interest rates that depend on the involved risk. Rates may range from 10% to over 25% annual rate of return (ARR).
  - Convertible debt designates loans that can or will convert into equity. The conversion may be triggered by a default in the payment schedule, by a specific point in time, or by some other event, as required by the investor. In the case of a default conversion, penalty or "clawback" provisions are commonly included, adding additional debt or equity expense to the deal.
  - Traditional bank note or a line of credit that is supported by the guarantee of a co-signature from an investor in exchange for equity, or more typically stock or unit warrants (options).
- Federal, state, regional or local governmental loans:
  - Small Business Administration (SBA) loans:
    - Loans directly available from the SBA
    - Loans available through traditional banks and guaranteed at some level by the SBA
  - Economic development-based loan programs. Most programs are targeted at specific industry types or geographic locations. Rates can vary from

very low to being comparable to a bank.

- Grant funding offers financing for specific advancement or improvement purposes; generally it does not need to be repaid. Some examples include:
  - National Institutes of Health (NIH) or Small Business Innovation Research (SBIR) grants.
  - State or federal economic development grants specifically aimed at growth of a target industry or for disaster recovery.

In my experience of securing grant funding for many companies, the key to success is understanding two things:
  - First, what is the overall intent of the grant program? If the intent is to create particular jobs, in a specific industry, at a target wage, then you need to write an application that focuses heavily on those deliverables.
  - Second, how will the grant committee score your application? Will they score it objectively based upon how well you filled out the application? Will it be rated upon criteria that was not explained in the application? Many grant committees have key "hot buttons" that are not explained, and if you want to be successful, you will need to learn these interests prior to submission. Talk to previous awardees, those who were rejected, or directly to review committee members.

The key to securing grants is the same as securing all other funding - you must understand the rules and involved personalities and then present your business and request in line with that view. I have seen grant committees make awards based on criteria not listed in the applications or supporting documents. I have seen many businesses follow all instructions, only to be turned down for reasons that were not explained.

If you want to be successful at securing grant funding, I would strongly suggest that you find an expert who has experience securing the specific grant for which you are applying and enlist their help. Like all funding, there is a science and an art to the process and in many cases, little to do with being "fair."

- Equity funding. Funding secured by selling equity in your business in the form of stock (S-corp. / C-corp.) or units (LLC's / Partnerships). (See below)

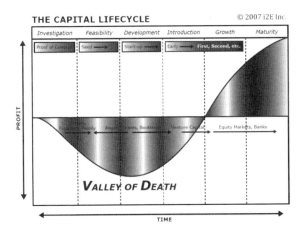

Raising Capital

Raising equity capital is a process that requires expert preparation, expertise and execution. Whether you are raising early-stage (seed-stage) start-up capital or business expansion (acceleration) capital, if you need other people's money to build your business, you need to be prepared.

This graphic[35] outlines the traditional investment stages, as well as sources of capital associated with each stage.

Start-up funding that you raise from friends, family, and local "angel investors" tends to be very patient money, gathered with more of an emotional, investment decision process. Friends and family believe in you, love you, and support you, regardless of the viability of the investment.

"Angel investors," usually high net-worth individuals who want to participate in something local, and perhaps have a family connection, may also make investments emotionally, based upon the novelty of the product and enthusiasm for and of the entrepreneur.

In most cases, these investors tend to believe you and spend little time truly understanding the detail, validity, and risk / reward potential of the investment. Many may write checks based solely upon the entrepreneur's enthusiasm and then ask for no supporting paperwork. The nice aspect about these investors is that they are usually very patient and passive in their overall involvement. However they rarely provide any quality hands-on help in the growth of your business, and typically, do not invest additional dollars if you get in trouble and need more.

"Angel Funds" or "Seed Funds" managed by an investment club or an ad-hoc group (neither having professional, full-time management) are the next level of investment. These people can invest larger amounts, and in most cases, perform a greater level of due diligence on the commitment. However, because the members of the fund usually have other full-time professions and are not seasoned investors, the amount of due diligence is limited. These investments also tend to have a strong emotional component.

The clear advantage to emotional investing is that you can raise some money without having an exceptionally polished "deal." The disadvantage of getting this "easier money" is that you may assume your deal is well polished when it is NOT. With these approaches, you are not forced to do the required work that will improve your odds of success. You are clearly not ready to look to professionally managed funds for additional capital, and if you try, you will get rejected. You will be asked questions that you cannot answer, and will be confused as to why these investors didn't get "excited" like the last ones. You will get frustrated and write them off saying, "They just don't get it." You will look for other fund investors, and find out that they must all "not get it" because none are interested. In actuality, your business "Recipe" is incomplete.

Professionally managed funds, whether they are seed, early-stage or later-stage venture capital funds, are in the game of investing for one reason - to make money with their money. These entities have full-time dedicated staff that expect passion as a given, and invest in deals that are wrapped and supported professionally. Great business ideas that have a solid "Strategic Fit" in the market, have a complete and believable business plan, and the right balance of talent and leadership get funded.

Typical seed stage capital requests begin with "I have this great idea for a product or service." Then they skip everything you have read in this book, go right to this point, and say, "Now all is need is the money." Everyday around the globe, there is an early-stage entrepreneur asking for capital armed only with a "great idea" or first-level prototype and his or her enthusiasm.

One of two things happens. Either an emotional investor or a family member is affected by the novelty of the deal and a passion for the entrepreneur and a small investment is made, or no investment is made. If the first scenario occurs, the deal will move forward without the "Recipe" needed to maximize success. If no investment is made, the entrepreneur will adopt the attitude that a lack of capital is keeping him or her from success. In either case, the entrepreneur has not yet learned that the necessary "Recipe" for building and operating a successful business is also the key to raising capital.

If you look at the "Report Card" you are completing in this book, the process is simple. If you want quality investment partners to help you start, accelerate, or buy a business, you need high marks in the first four categories. If you want to secure and manage a quality banking relationship or secure applicable grants, you need the same results.

Securing proper resources is completely a function of having the right ingredients and execution capabilities. The more of both elements that you do not have, the harder it will be to secure the needed resources. The formula is simple; the execution is hard work. The result from a great "Recipe" is a significantly improved chance of success.

RECIPE CHECK: RESOURCES

- The quality and amount of resources you are able to employ will significantly impact your ability to execute.
- Your ability to gather the appropriate resources is a direct result of your ability to build the right "Recipe."
- Critical resource types include: information, technical, human, environmental, and financial.

- Not all banks or investors are interchangeable; do your research and engage the right ones in a worthwhile way.
- When considering bank debt:
  - Banks take low levels of risk
  - Banks require collateral
  - The better the "Recipe," the better the loan terms
- When considering raising investor funding:
  - Personal investors can, and do, make personal investment decisions
  - Fund investors make considered, business decisions
  - The better the "Recipe," the better the valuation and terms

SCORE YOUR BUSINESS

At this point, take a moment and score your business on page 185. If you can truly say that you have all the resources outlined herein, score yourself at ten. If you can identify some of the resources, but still need to secure others, score yourself accordingly. Your scoring will allow you to identify opportunities for improved performance, so grade yourself honestly.

SECTION 3

REPORT CARD

REPORT CARD

Identifying Opportunities for Improvement

We have worked through a quality "Recipe" for a successful business. To make maximum use of the presented materials, it is essential that you take an uncolored, unemotional look at your business, or business model, and score it accordingly.

Using the provided "Report Card," honestly rate your business based upon the "Recipe" presented in this book. Higher numbers indicate a greater amount of each ingredient or execution component. The higher the overall score, the easier it will be for your business to excel. The lower the number, the greater the opportunity you will have for improvement.

Strategic Fit: You need a viable and defendable reason to be in business or to start a business.

Business Plan: If you have a viable reason, but do not have a plan, your chances of success are limited.

Talent: If you have a plan, but are missing a balanced team to execute it, you will perform accordingly.

Leadership: You simply cannot build and retain a quality team or business without the right leadership.

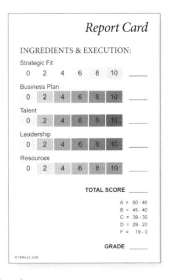

Report Card

INGREDIENTS & EXECUTION:

Strategic Fit
0 2 4 6 8 10 _____

Business Plan
0 2 4 6 8 10 _____

Talent
0 2 4 6 8 10 _____

Leadership
0 2 4 6 8 10 _____

Resources
0 2 4 6 8 10 _____

TOTAL SCORE _____

A = 50 - 46
B = 45 - 40
C = 39 - 30
D = 29 - 20
F = 19 - 0

GRADE _____

© CRN LLC 2009

Resources: You cannot execute well without the proper resources. If you have the above items, your resources will be much easier to identify and secure. Businesses with high scores in the first four categories are funded faster and at higher valuations!

RECIPE CHECK: YOUR RECIPE

Few, if any, will ever score an "A" or be able to objectively claim to be in perfect balance. Realizing where you have balance issues and working toward perfection is the mark of a great business and, likely, a strong business leader.

High-performance results come from executing in balance with the proper ingredients and capabilities:

Proper ingredients:
- Strategic Fit:
    - Viable Need
    - Viable Opportunity
    - Viable Product
    - Viable Pricing
    - Viable Operation
    - Viable Environment
- Business Plan:
    - Executive Summary
    - Things Learned
    - Function and Scope
    - Mission and Principles
    - Strategic Fit
    - Assumptions and Critical Issues
    - Strengths and Weaknesses
    - Objectives and Goals
    - Strategies and Tactics
    - Operations Plans
    - Financials and Resources
    - Monitoring Plan
    - Action Plan

Proper execution capabilities:
- Talent:
  - Disciplines
  - Capability and Experience
  - Balance
- Leadership:
  - Experienced and Capable
- Resources:
  - Information
  - Technology
  - Human
  - Environmental
  - Financial

Just like any other type of recipe, less-than-optimal to poor results come from executing out of balance in any one or more of the required components. Can you operate out of balance and still remain viable? There are businesses that make such happen, every day. Many businesses last a generation or more while running out of balance. Can you come to believe that your out-of-balance business is completely in balance? It would seem that most businesses operate in this mode, "not knowing what they don't know." These owners and executives do not assess their "Recipe" because they like the one they have.

John was eight years old and had a passion for chocolate cake. His mother made him chocolate cake every Saturday after he finished his chores. At this point in his life, he had only tasted his mother's cake and had loved it.

One day he was playing at his friend Sam's house. Sam's mother yelled out to them and asked if they would like some chocolate cake and milk. Needless to say, John responded with an immediate, "yes." When he went inside, he was confronted by a five-layer chocolate cake with homemade chocolate frosting. It is important to note that the chocolate cake John's mother always made was a one-inch thick sheet cake with canned frosting.

The first thing John said to Sam's mother was," What's that?" She said, "It's chocolate cake." John said, "No, my mom makes chocolate cake and that is not what this is." Sam's mother finally convinces him that this was simply a different type of chocolate cake, and once he took a bite, John was blown away by how good it was. He now had a much different perspective on chocolate cake and realized that the cake he had been eating all his life was not the best that was available.

When it comes to your business, ask yourself these simple questions:

- Do you focus on how good your business is?
- Or do you focus on how much better it could be?

Driving Continuous Improvement

The process of creating and maintaining a quality business "Recipe" is ongoing. You will never assemble all ingredients or execution components in perfect balance. There will always be challenges and opportunities. The key to maximizing success over the long term is continuous analysis and constant execution of "Recipe" improving actions.

Please use the information in this book, as well as your report card, to continually analyze and improve your business. I urge you to build a better business for you, your family, your employees and their families, and for your regional and national economy.

REPORT CARD

If you build a quality "Recipe" for your business, award-winning results will follow.

Report Card

INGREDIENTS & EXECUTION:

Strategic Fit

| 0 | 2 | 4 | 6 | 8 | 10 | _____ |

Business Plan

| 0 | 2 | 4 | 6 | 8 | 10 | _____ |

Talent

| 0 | 2 | 4 | 6 | 8 | 10 | _____ |

Leadership

| 0 | 2 | 4 | 6 | 8 | 10 | _____ |

Resources

| 0 | 2 | 4 | 6 | 8 | 10 | _____ |

TOTAL SCORE _____

A = 50 - 46
B = 45 - 40
C = 39 - 30
D = 29 - 20
F = 19 - 0

GRADE _____

© CRN LLC 2009

THE RECIPE FOR BUSINESS SUCCESS:

DOCUMENTED RESOURCES

[1] Finegan, J., & Hofman, M. (1997, October 21). Inc 500. Inc, 19(15), 145-161.

[2] Chicotel, S., & McLaughlin, S. (1998, October 15). The list 500. Inc, 20(15), 81-96.

[3] Hofman, M., & Borrego, A. (1999, October 19). Inc. 500. Inc, 21(15), 121-137.

[4] Armstrong, J.W. (2001, September 25). US Patent 6293874 --User-operated amusement apparatus for kicking the user's buttocks. Available from U.S. Patent and Trademark Office site: http://patft.uspto.gov/

NOTE: Featured illustration is drawn from inventor's patent application and is visible within application narrative.

[5] See the following, original research proposing the adoption cycle:

Bohlen, J. M., & Beal, G. M. (1957, May). The diffusion process. Special Report No. 18 (*Agriculture Extension Service, Iowa State College*), 56–77. Retrieved from: http://www.soc.iastate.edu/extension/presentations/publications/comm/Diffusion%20Process.pdf

Rogers, E.M. (1962). *Diffusion of innovations*. New York, NY: The Free Press of Glencoe, 1962.

Graphic of the "Everett Rogers' Technology Adoption Lifecycle model," also known as "Diffusion of Innovations," is available online from various resources. Sample site offering:

Technology adoption lifecycle. (n.d.). In *Wikipedia*: The Free Encyclopedia. Retrieved August 16, 2009, from http://en.wikipedia.org/wiki/Technology_adoption_lifecycle

[6] Moore, G. (1999). *Crossing the chasm*. (2nd ed.). Oxford, England: Capstone, 1999.

Moore, G. (2002). *Crossing the chasm: marketing and selling disruptive products to mainstream customers*. (rev.ed.). New York, NY: HarperBusiness Essentials, 2002.

[7] See the 3M Corporation website for details on the notes' creation.

THE RECIPE FOR BUSINESS SUCCESS

3M. (2009). *3M:Post-It: The Whole Story*. Retrieved from http://www.3m.com/us/office/postit/pastpresent/history_ws.html

[8] Discussion with Robert Hoke and Ryan Carter; Nymaster, Goode, West, Hansell, and O'Brien, P.C., Cedar Rapids, IA.

[9] For further details about AOL's (American Online) company history, visit:

Wikipedia. (2009). *AOL*. Retrieved August 5, 2009, from http://en.wikipedia.org/wiki/AOL

[10] Cowley, M., & Domb, E. (1997). *Beyond strategic vision: effective corporate action with Hoshin planning*. Boston, MA: Butterworth-Heinemann.

[11] Sony Corporation 1950's mission statement is indirectly referenced in numerous websites. To view the current mission statement of Wal-Mart, see:

Wal-Mart. (2009) *Investor Frequently Asked Questions*. Retrieved August 10, 2009, from http://walmartstores.com/Investors/7614.aspx.

[12] See December 2005 narrative of the genesis of the SWOT analysis by Albert Humphrey, alumnus of the Stanford Research Institute (SRI).

Humphrey, S. A. (2005, December). *December 2005 Newsletter: History Corner: SWOT Analysis for Management Consulting*. SRI Alumni Association Newsletter, pp. 7-8. Retrieved from http://alumni.sri.com/newsletters/Dec-05.pdf

[13] S.M.A.R.T. goals have been often attributed to both Kenneth Blanchard and Paul J. Meyer. For one of the earliest instances of SMART noted in a professional journal, see:

Doran, G.T. (1981, November). There's a S.M.A.R.T. way to write management's goals and objectives. *Management Review*, 70(11), 35-36.

[14] Reis, A., & Reis, L. (2002). *The fall of advertising and the rise of PR*. New York, NY: HarperBusiness.

[15] Various sources point to the debacle involved in the "60 Minutes" broadcast. See the following:

Huber, P. (1989, December 18). Manufacturing the Audi scare. *Wall Street Journal* (New York, NY), Eastern ed., p.1.

[16] To see the "50 Worst Cars of All Time" list, and the Cimarron's position as a 1982 selection, consult the following:

The 50 Worst Cars of All Time. Retrieved August 10, 2009, from http://www.time.com/time/specials/2007/completelist/0,,1658545,00.html

DOCUMENTED RESOURCES

Levitt, S. D. (2009, August 4). *The 50 worst cars of all time: Freakonomics: the hidden side of everything. The New York Times*. Retrieved August 10, 2009, from http://freakonomics.blogs.nytimes.com/2009/08/04/the-50-worst-cars-of-all-time/

[17] For discussion of the VW Phaeton, visit:

Car Talk: Test Drive Notes: 2004 VW Phaeton. Retrieved from http://www.cartalk.com/content/testdrives/Reviews/vw-phaeton-2004.html

Consumer Guide Automotive. *2006 Volkswagen Phaeton: Overview*. Retrieved from http://consumerguideauto.howstuffworks.com/2006-volkswagen-phaeton.htm

Edmunds.com. *2006 Volkswagen Phaeton Review*. Retrieved from http://www.edmunds.com/volkswagen/phaeton/2006/review.html

[18] To visit the websites of the noted companies, consider the following.
(a). *Sweetwater*: Music Instruments & Pro Audio. Available: http://www.sweetwater.com
(b). *Crutchfield: North America's Electronic Specialist Since 1974*. Available: http://www.crutchfield.com
(c). *Tirerack: Performance Experts for Tires and Wheels*. Available: http://www.tirerack.com/.
(d) *Johnston & Murphy*. Available: http://www.johnstonmurphy.com/

[19] Discussion with Steven Schoenauer; RSM McGladrey; Cedar Rapids, Iowa.

[20] The American Marketing Association offers a recent definition (2007) on its website. Please consult the following resource:

MarketingPower, Inc. (2009). *American Marketing Association; About AMA: Definition of Marketing*. Retrieved from http://www.marketingpower.com/AboutAMA/Pages/DefinitionofMarketing.aspx

[21] Hopkins,T. (1980). *How to master the art of selling*. New York, NY: Warner Books.

Tom Hopkins International. (2008). *Tom Hopkins International: The Builder of Sales Champions*. Retrieved from http://www.tomhopkins.com/

[22] Business books and resources noted in this paragraph include:

Miller, R., Heiman, S., & Tuleja, T. (1985). *Strategic selling: the unique sales system proven successful by America's best companies*. New York, NY: W. Morrow.

NOTE: New editions in 1988, 1998; revised and updated in 2005

Rackham, N. (1989). *Major account sales strategy*. New York, NY: McGraw-Hill.

Rackham, N. (1988). *SPIN selling*. New York, NY: McGraw-Hill.

For further information about Joe Golding, President and CEO of Differentiation Strategies, Inc., please visit the following:

Differentiation Strategies, Inc. (2009). *DiffStrat: Creating the change you want to see*. Retrieved from http://www.diffstrat.com/

[23] See Reid, P.C. citation following.

[24] Reid, P.C. *Well made in America: Lessons from Harley-Davidson on being the best*. New York, NY: McGraw-Hill, 1990.

[25] Meyer, N. (Director). (1982). *Star Trek II: The Wrath of Khan* [DVD]. Hollywood, CA: Paramount.

[26] Full job website addresses are as follows: (1) http://www.monster.com; (2) http://www.careerbuilder.com; (3) http://www.dice.com; and (4) http://hotjobs.yahoo.com. The popular search engine, Google, is located at http://www.google.com.

[27] Noted, social media websites of interest include: (1) http://www.linkedin.com; (2) http://twitter.com ; and (3) http://www.facebook.com.

[28] The DISC Assessment is a psychological inventory that measures behavior styles and performance in a given environment; the test was developed by John Geier. The Myers-Briggs Type Indicator (MBTI) determines personality type, while the Caliper Profile measures job-related potential, motivation, and other employee qualities.

[29] Discussion with Cindy Lyness, Management Recruiters of Cedar Rapids; Cedar Rapids, Iowa, and Laura Higgins, Caliper Corporation; Virginia Beach, Virginia

[30] Gerstner, L. (2002). *Who says elephants can't dance*? : inside IBM's historic turnaround. New York, NY: HarperBusiness.

[31] For further details about Pure Fishing's company history, visit the following:

Bruggom, M. (2007, April 10). *Radio Iowa News: Former Iowa Congressman's company, Pure Fishing, sold*. Retrieved August 10, 2009, from http://www.radioiowa.com/gestalt/go.cfm?objectid=DC53DCBA-9C50-C5E5-A18D38254AE4CDD1

Pure Fishing. (2009). *Our Rich History: The only big fish story that's true from start to finish*. Retrieved from http://www.berkley-fishing.com/about_history.php

DOCUMENTED RESOURCES

[32] Sandberg, former Vice President of Global Online Sales and Operations at Google (2001-2007), is now Chief Operating Officer (COO) at Facebook. For details on the Google episode, visit:

Kotelnikvo, V. (n.d.) *Freedom to Fail: The Highway to Success.* Retrieved August 16, 2009, from http://www.1000ventures.com/business_guide/crosscuttings/failure_freedom.html

For further details on Sandberg's current activities, please see the following:

Schwartz, B. (2008, May 4). *Facebook's New Chief Operating Officer, Ex-Google VP, Sandberg.* Retrieved from http://searchengineland.com/facebooks-new-chief-operating-officer-ex-google-vp-sandberg-13505

Press Room: Executive Bios: Facebook. (2009). Retrieved August 10, 2009, from http://www.facebook.com/press/info.php?execbios

[33] Sargent, C. (2006). *From buddy to boss: effective fire service leadership.* Tulsa, OK: PennWellCorp.

[34] For further details about Schuler, visit his consulting business, Schuler Solutions, Inc.

Schuler, A.J. (n.d.). *Schuler Solutions, Inc.* Retrieved from http://www.schuler-solutions.com/.

Schuler, A.J. (2003). *Leadership Self Test.* Retrieved from http://www.schulersolutions.com/html/leadership_self_test.html

[35] "The Capital Lifecycle" graphic was featured in a 2007 multimedia presentation, sponsored by i2E, the facilitating organization for the Oklahoma Technology Commercialization Center (OTCC) in Oklahoma City. Attribution for the graphic follows:

i2E, Inc. (2009). i2E: *Turning Innovation into Enterprise.* Retrieved August 16, 2009 from http://www.i2e.org/DesktopDefault.aspx

THE RECIPE FOR BUSINESS SUCCESS:

SUPPLEMENTAL SOURCES

NOTE: Please visit the "Recipe for Business Success" website (http:///www.recipeforbusinesssuccess.com) for the following resources:

- Business plan outline
- Marketing plan outline
- Team scoring charts
- Job description samples
- Interview form samples
- Expanded answers to A.J. Shuler's leadership quiz
- Product development flow chart
- Sales process flow-chart
- Sales funnel templates
- Suggested reading materials
- Future enhancements

1. The "Product Life Cycle" is referenced and diagrammed in numerous sources. A sampling of such locations includes the following website: http://samueljscott.files.wordpress.com/2007/09/product-life-cycle.png

2. Consulted professionals and experts who assisted with this project, in order of appearance, include:

- Robert W. Hoke; Nymaster, Goode, West, Hansell, & O'Brien, P.C., Cedar Rapids, Iowa
- Ryan N. Carter; Nymaster, Goode, West, Hansell, & O'Brien, P.C., Cedar Rapids, Iowa
- Drew McLellan; McLellan Marketing Group, Des Moines, Iowa
- Steven Schoenauer; Managing Partner, RSM McGladrey, Cedar Rapids, Iowa
- Cindy Lyness; Owner, Management Recruiters of Cedar Rapids; Cedar Rapids, Iowa
- Laura Higgins; Caliper Corporation
- Larry Helling; President and CEO, Cedar Rapids Bank & Trust (CRB&T), Cedar Rapids, Iowa
- Paul Rhines; Principal, AAVIN Venture Partners; Cedar Rapids, Iowa
- Anne King; Lecturer, Department of Business, Mount Mercy College, Cedar Rapids, Iowa
- Julie Zielinski; Consultant, Entrepreneurial Development Center, Inc. (EDC), Cedar Rapids, Iowa, and Business Director of the MBA Marketing Academy, University of Iowa, Iowa City, Iowa

- Maureen Szlemp; Marketing and Communications Consultant
- Peter Fry; Adjunct Professor, Kaplan University
- Josie Heskje; VP Marketing, Entrepreneurial Development Center, Inc., Cedar Rapids, IA

3. To view guidelines and details of governance for the Meredith Corporation, please visit:

   Corporate Governance, Meredith Corporation. (n.d.). Retrieved August 16, 2009, from http://www.meredith.com/meredith_corporate/gov_guidelines.html

4. Content from the 1970, Academy Award winning feature film, *Patton*, is taken from the following media:

   Schaffner, F.J. (Director). (2006). *Patton* [DVD] Beverly Hills, CA: Twentieth Century Fox Home Entertainment.

5. Information regarding the competitive value matrix can be obtained thusly:

MarketValueSolutions. (2008). *Competitive Value Matrix: Find Your Value Proposition.* Retrieved from http://marketvaluesolutions.com/competitive-value-matrix.htm